Praise for Spirit Walking

M000290603

"Evelyn Rysdyk brings the reader face to face with the bones of reality—how it works in this Middle World—and how the practice of shamanism helps us to live in good relationship with *All That Is*. Embracing the venerable worldview of shamanism, she compassionately guides readers on their own journey of discovery and empowerment within the reality of an ensouled Universe. *Spirit Walking* is comprehensive and inspiring—Evelyn's outstanding artistry is evocatively expressed through her writings as well as images. A most worthy read!"

—Nan Moss and David Corbin, authors of *Weather Shamanism: Harmonizing Our Connection with the Elements*

"What I love about reading Evelyn Rysdyk is her ability to combine ancient lore with modern science so seamlessly that you would swear you can't have one without the other. With the lyrical voice of an artist she taps into our memories of old, 'forgotten' ways and helps us understand them in terms of the latest findings in physics, psychology, and ecology. She is a wonderful guide for spirit walking between the worlds. Walk with her."

—Tom Cowan, author of *Fire in the Head* and *Yearning for the Wind*

"In our ever-changing world many people feel lost and isolated within their lives. Through *Spirit Walking* Evelyn Rysdyk uses her grace and gifts to help shift our connection to the earth, each other and ourselves, building the foundation for life in a new and different world. She is an exceptional writer, artist, healer and human 'being.'"

—Joan Emmons, publisher of *Inner Tapestry*

"Life is a sacred work . . . How easy it is to forget that in the rush of daily life! And how wonderful it is when a book like this comes along, not only reminding us of our deepest sense of connection and purpose, but offering wise guidance to help us get back to it."

—Hillary S. Webb, author of *Traveling between the Worlds: Conversations with Contemporary Shamans*

"An inspiring and critically important work, this book helps you use all of the spiritual tools and connections you were born with, but most likely forgot. *Spirit Walking* clearly explains what shamanism is and does, while teaching in a concise, step-by-step, fashion how to bring this way of being into your everyday life. I loved that I could feel the profound wisdom of many years of experience flow through Evelyn's writing in such a personal way. It feels like she is teaching you directly, with all her deeply rooted energy and spirit guided words. Whether you are new to shamanism, or are living this way of life already, you will find this book a valuable resource. At a time when life can seem so crazy, we need to become Spirit Walkers now, more than ever!"

—Colleen Deatsman, author of *The Hollow Bone: A Field Guide to Shamanism* and *Seeing in the Dark: Claim Your Own Shamanic Power Now and in the Coming Age*

"Evelyn Rysdyk has written an invaluable shamanic resource that is at once expansive and concise. She shares her deep wisdom with humility and great generosity of spirit."

—Mama Donna Henes, urban shaman, author and spirituality columnist for the Huffington Post, Beliefnet, and UPI

Spirit Walking

A Course in Shamanic Power

Evelyn C. Rysdyk

WEISER BOOKS
San Francisco, CA / Newburyport, MA

First published in 2013 by Weiser Books
Red Wheel/Weiser, LLC
With offices at:
665 Third Street, Suite 400
San Francisco, CA 94107
www.redwheelweiser.com

ISBN: 978-1-57863-541-2

Library of Congress Cataloging-in-Publication data available upon request

Cover design by Jim Warner
Cover image: Drumming at the Edge of the Cosmos, digital art © Evelyn Rysdyk, with special thanks to Sven Geier, *www.sgeier.net*, for his Kappa Space fractal
Interior by Dutton & Sherman
Typeset in Sabon and Frutiger text and Nueva display

Printed in the United States of America
MAL

10 9 8 7 6 5 4 3 2 1

The paper used in this publication meets the minimum requirements of the American National Standard for Information Sciences—Permanence of Paper for Printed Library Materials Z39.48-1992 (R1997).

Contents

Foreword

In the Western world we try to think our way out of problems; we attempt to come up with a plan. The trouble is, the problems we have created in this world—war, greed, inequality of resources, feelings of scarcity, and fear—are often beyond a rational plan of action. We need to look both deeper and further for answers.

When we take time to reflect deeply on our lives, we notice that often an invisible hand, the divine, the spiritual forces of the universe have brought us out of a dark place into a place of healing or one where good things start to manifest. Those spiritual forces know how to create the transformation we are seeking. The more we can call in spirit and let it move in ways that are beyond our rational comprehension, the more we open the doorway for this to happen, both on a personal and planetary level. This is the way of the shaman.

In *Spirit Walking: A Course in Shamanic Power,* Evelyn Rysdyk brilliantly shares with us a means of practicing shamanism and tapping into this powerful ancient tradition for guidance and healing. Rather than focusing our thoughts and our imaginations on our challenges and troubles, which only ends up feeding them, we must practice using our imaginations to dream about a world that embraces love, peace, light, abundance, and equality for all.

We must dream it into being. In *Spirit Walking*, Evelyn teaches you how to do just that.

Spirit Walking addresses how when we step into the imaginal world of the shaman we discover a true richness of life. We learn how to once again regain the depth of senses, to hear our inner music, and to remember the preciousness of life. We start to wake up from the collective trance that keeps us from experiencing our deep inner world. And as we strengthen our connection to spirit and begin to create a new fabric of reality in the invisible realms, we begin to see it manifest into the physical world to replace all that is unraveling.

In this book Evelyn walks you through many practices that will connect you with the world of spirit and give you ways to call on the spirits for help. She brings a fresh perspective to the work by showing how the latest findings in quantum physics are verifying what the shamans have always known, namely that all matter is energy, that all matter has consciousness, and that we are all connected in a far more intricate web of energy and spirit than we have been led to believe. She shares powerful stories of shamans from a variety of cultures such as Nepalese, Tuvan, the Ulchi from Siberia, and from Peru. She helps us see how we can learn from indigenous teachers and integrate shamanic practices into our own lives. What I especially appreciate about Evelyn is that she is not a voyeur. It's easy to think we can simply copy what indigenous shamans do and get the same results. But of course that's not the way things work. Evelyn knows that deeply. She has delved into the practices herself and has made them her own, and she will show you how to walk a path that is enriched by the ways of the shaman and still authentic to your life and experience.

Evelyn takes away some of the mystery of shamanic work with her clear explanations and step-by-step instructions. And her original art, which is used throughout the book, not only inspires us but also imbues the work with special power.

Read *Spirit Walking* and learn from this master teacher. Read, reflect, devote yourself to the practices she teaches, and you too can become a spirit walker.

—SANDRA INGERMAN, AUTHOR OF *SHAMANIC JOURNEYING: A BEGINNER'S GUIDE* AND *THE SHAMAN'S TOOLKIT: ANCIENT TOOLS FOR SHAPING THE LIFE AND WORLD YOU WANT TO LIVE IN*

Acknowledgments

I wish to acknowledge our clients whose courage has filled me with awe, our students for their excitement, energy, and input, which helps me to be an ever-better teacher—and to all the journeying shamans who have paved my way.

This book is dedicated to all my teachers in ordinary reality and in the spirit realms. I recognize the profound blessings I have received from the spirits of the Earth, my power animals, teachers, and ancestors. I offer a special heartfelt acknowledgment of the loving guidance and protection I have received from my Great, Great Grandma Henderer and Bear.

I offer deep gratitude to the many fine human teachers with whom I have been blessed to study. I choose to especially honor here Ai Churek, Roy Bauer, Gregg Braden, Grandfather Mikhail "Misha" Duvan, Nadyezda Duvan, Michael Harner, Sandra Harner, Sandra Ingerman, the Institute of HeartMath, Marrianna Konbou, Brooke Medicine Eagle, Fredy "Puma" Quispe Singona, and David Reilly, MD. Special thanks also to my dear friend, Bhola N. Banstola, my shamanic colleagues of URSA, my agent Stephany Evans of FinePrint Literary Management, Trudy Sloan for sharing her wonderful poetry in these pages, Aisha Saidi for being a rigorous, spirited, and patient editor, and Caroline Pincus of Red Wheel/Weiser for choosing to publish this volume.

Lastly and most importantly, I honor the loving blessings I receive from my wonderful family, my dear friends, and my incredible life partner, Allie Knowlton, who is a wealth of heart wisdom and always a ready coconspirator!

Disclaimer

I wrote this book to support you in developing a personal practice of shamanism. The suggestions, therapeutic processes, and shamanic techniques described in this book are in no way meant to replace professional medical or mental health assistance. Please consult a medical professional for any persistent condition. In addition, while this program offers rituals to heal you, this book does not replace formal instruction in shamanic healing on behalf of others. No one should attempt the techniques in this book on another person without such training. To do so could bring serious harm to your patient as well as you.

Introduction

While many people are fascinated by the ways of the shaman, few people feel that they are able to access genuine spiritual power themselves. This book is meant to help each of you awaken your inherent spiritual abilities and make connections with the boundless energies that animate the cosmos. By following the methods presented in these pages, you can become a person who dances along the shaman's path between this world and that of the spirits—a "spirit walker!"

Shamanism is an ancient spiritual practice rooted in the ideas that all matter has consciousness and that accessing the spirit in all things is part of what keeps the world and people healthy, in balance, and in harmony. The spirit beings that surround us are also the source of a spirit walker's ability to profoundly influence life events and thrive in difficult circumstances.

My own difficult situation led me to explore the ways of the shaman. In my thirties, I experienced a profound depression. The light and joy drained from my life. While I worked with a counselor and took medication to allow me to sleep, neither these nor my strength of will was enough to lift me out of the darkness. Being deeply depressed is like being a horse wearing blinders. Your world narrows to a sliver of its former richness. You lose all ability to perceive the full depth and breadth of life.

While searching for ways to recover my confidence and vitality, I found an advertisement for a workshop with anthropologist Michael Harner about the Way of the Shaman. After a half day of his delightful stories, Michael led me into my first shamanic journey experience. As soon as I entered the world of the spirits, something astonishing occurred. I had the extraordinary feeling of possibilities rushing back to me. They weren't specific notions, just the sense that opportunities, ideas, and desires were suddenly feasible again.

That moment set my feet on the spirit walker's path. I read, took workshops, studied with tribal shamans, but most importantly, I entered into relationships with a power animal and spirit teacher. Over the next twenty years, I came to understand what these affiliations provided. These relationships with spirits altered my ways of interacting with other people, other beings, and my environment. I was changed and discovered that these connections were the true source of power.

A spirit walker or shamanic practitioner chooses to be a special kind of person. This individual chooses to be in right relationship with All That Is and thus is able to access the powers that flow around us. The spirit walker accesses these powers for the good of all beings—for healing, gaining insight, getting guidance, and generally making life better. The shamanic rituals, healings, and journeys that the spirit walker performs are grounded in methods that have endured for millennia around the globe. But despite their long history, these methods offer fresh approaches, which can support you in regaining your vitality and renewing the energy in your life right now. As you wend your way along this journey of deep connection, you will be supported in remembering your own intrinsic preciousness as well.

In living a more powerful, healthier, and more loving life, you will affect the other people whom your life touches. Your positive shifts will become healing ripples throughout the entire web of life. In my years of doing this work and helping many people find their way along this path, I have come to believe that this is how the world can and will be healed. It all begins with one extraordinary being—you—feeling the power of connection with the entire fabric of existence!

Shamanic spirituality has always been intimately connected to survival. At its origins with our ancient ancestors, the shaman's efforts helped the tribal group successfully negotiate a healthy path through the perils of both the seen and unseen worlds. Whether through locating the migrating herds of animals on which the people depended for sustenance or tending to the sick with songs and medicinal plants, the shaman's skill was necessary to support people's lives.

Figure 1. Grandfather Mikhail "Misha" Duvan, the last male shaman of the Ulchi of Siberia, in his ritual garb. Pen and ink.

The survival of our species may once again depend on those who choose to follow the shaman's path. We human beings have made it this far because of our interconnection and interdependence on each other and other species. The more deeply we explore these especially delicate interconnections—the strands that create the fabric of life on Earth—the more awestruck and humbled we become. Unfortunately, many people are unable to see or feel these bonds, often exploiting the richness and beauty of the Earth in a vain effort to gain power.

You are reading this because you think and feel differently. You are willing to remember your authentic, power-filled self. You understand that each of us is intimately connected to everything else. You may also have a sense that the shamanic way can give you a much-needed bridge back to balance and joy. While it may not be possible to fully reclaim the ancient lifestyle that gave birth to the first shamans, it is possible to reconnect with your own power and with your ancestors' understanding of the precious nature of all beings.

Throughout this book, you will be given exercises and questions to consider to deepen your experience. Take your time, answer the questions as honestly as you can, and follow through with each of the exercises: they are meant to support your evolution into a spirit walker. This is an essential part of any shamanic path. The spirit walker follows an inward journey of growing personal power, even as she or he develops awareness of and connections to the spiritual power that is all around.

To make sure you get the most benefit from these exercises and questions, dedicate a notebook or journal to the work of this book. This will be of invaluable assistance in helping you fully internalize all that you will learn in these pages. The audio files you will need and other resources to support your exploration may be found at *www.myspiritwalk.com*. A companion book, *A Spirit Walker's Guide to Shamanic Implements,* is also available through the site.

You will also notice that the terms *spirit walker* and *shaman* have different meanings in this book. A shaman is a healer—often indigenous—who is recognized as such by her or his community. I use the term spirit walker or shamanic practitioner to distinguish the essence of what it means to be a shaman apart from the role within the community. That is, you not only walk between the realms to access the spiritual, you also walk alongside the spirits of nature and your helping spirits. It is these relationships with spirits, animals, birds, plants, natural forces, and other human beings that provide a fresh way to be in harmony with All That Is.

So, as it has been in the distant past, the spirit walker's path—your path—is about creating a way to thrive in community. In deciding to walk with the spirits, you are choosing to reclaim the magic that people lost along the way to the twenty-first century. Supported by the loving spirits of All That Is, who are whispering their encouragement, you will help weave a new future for yourself and our planet.

Now, let's embark on this marvelous, spirit-walking adventure together!

EVELYN C. RYSDYK
WWW.SPIRITPASSAGES.COM

The Search
I turn the pages
And wander through the centuries
In and out of great minds
Seeking answers.
I hope to pick up truth
A polished pebble for my pocket
Something solid to save,
Grasp in times of shaken need.
But truth is never pocket-sized,
Never solid.
The wise let truth carry them,
Content to be polished
By the ceaseless motion
Of its questions.

TRUDY SLOAN

Chapter 1

Unraveling the Mysteries

S hamanism has roots that extend very deeply into our collective human past. Originating in the time when people all over the globe lived as hunters and gatherers, shamanism is an ancient spiritual tradition that presupposes that the world around us is alive: the plants, trees, animals, birds, and people are filled with *spirit* that enlivens and animates them. Furthermore, the health and strength of any individual being is a direct reflection of the vitality of this animating force. During the subsequent spread of our species to every corner of the Earth, we carried this understanding of the world with us and incorporated it into our different tribal traditions. Observers of widely diverse shamanic cultures—from Africa to the Americas to Asia—see amazingly similar practices that clearly reflect our common spiritual origins.

Much of the malaise people experience in our contemporary world seems to originate from the perceived disconnection of our bodies, minds, and spirits. The greatest gifts the shamanic path can offer you are ways to access your innate wisdom while recalling your profound spiritual connection to *All That Is*. As my Spirit Teacher says, it is about you remembering your *"inherent preciousness."* Through relationships with helpful and healing spirits and the spirits of nature, you can recognize that you are "no more or less important than any other being in Creation and as a Divine being, you are both loved and Love itself."[1]

As you remember your relationship with All That Is, your perceptions will shift about who you are, why you are here, and how you can participate in the larger world. We create our understanding of what is real based upon our perceptions of the world. As you shift and change, your reality itself will be altered leading to real concrete changes in your life.

Most of what we know about the world is learned information. The very first education we receive is from the family in which we are raised and later from the larger culture in which our family exists. In other words, each of us was taught our conscious and subconscious definitions of reality. This process affects how we understand the world and ourselves. As we learn new definitions, we are capable of replacing our previously learned views with a more harmonious way of knowing.

As you connect more deeply with yourself, with the world of the spirits, and with nature, you will gain indisputable personal evidence to act as an antidote to the compartmentalized and isolating view of the world that has become prevalent during the past few centuries. As this happens, the limiting beliefs you were taught in your early life will begin to fade away. You will step back into a way of knowing held by your most ancient ancestors—that you are an integral part of the Circle of Life that holds us all.

The Shaman's Paradigm

While the shamanic view may be considered "primitive" today, modern science is discovering principles that support the ways our ancestors understood the world surrounding them. In the shamanic worldview, it isn't just the animals, birds, and plants that are alive; everything is spirit-filled. This concept is called animist. The word *animism*, first coined by English anthropologist Sir Edward Tylor in *Primitive Cultures* (1871), comes from the Latin *anima*, or soul.

Whether it is the plants, animals, birds, or even landscape features such as rivers and mountains or forces such as the wind and the rain—animists believe that each part of our environment has a vital essence or spirit and a consciousness. A shaman also understands that spirit is the framework on which physical existence is sustained. Spirit is at the foundation of everything, and it is the connective tissue of all aspects of our physical existence.

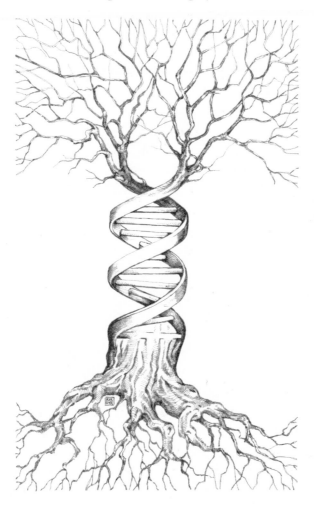

Figure 2. Tree of Life.

In quantum physics, the world is seen as originating in the vibrations created by infinitesimal superstrings. Each of these imperceptible features has the capacity to produce a particle of matter. In the paradigm of New Physics, this invisible and impalpable "something" connects all physical reality. Everything we think of as living, as well as those aspects of our world that we perceive as inanimate, are interlinked on the quantum level.

Even our own bodies' physicality reveals points of connection that our ancestors believed were an intrinsic feature of life. Today, we know that the elemental raw materials that compose our bodies, such as iron, calcium, oxygen, sodium, and all the rest, are the same materials that make up the mountains, seas, atmosphere, and soils of our planet.

Within every one of our cells, we carry the elemental building blocks of life—DNA—a remarkable double helix-shaped chain of chemical information that shapes our physical form. And housed within the twisting steps of this amazing molecule is the story of our evolution as human beings. What is truly astounding is that we share 90 percent of our genetic material with other species. Everything from the bear to the oak tree to the tiniest bacteria has the same four amino acids making up their bodies. Recent discoveries have documented the fact that inside of the 60,000 to 80,000 genes that constitute our human genome lies the information to create all other life-forms on the planet. When molecular biologists examine the complex strands of our DNA, they also find housed within it more than a blueprint for a human being, but rather an extraordinary library of codes for all life on Earth. We carry the entire interlinked biosphere in every cell. We are part of all of Creation and all of Creation is held within us.[2]

In addition to being an extraordinary storehouse of information, the structure of our DNA is also a source of measurable energy. Studies in the 1980s determined that DNA emits photons in the visible light range (900-200 nanometer), which although weak, exhibit a laser-like coherency.[3] Photons are particles of light matter having no mass; they may be proven by physics, but not weighed in the traditional manner.[4] They are normally imperceptible to our senses, yet they are constantly radiating from the DNA in every cell. A remarkable property of a photon is that, since it has no measurable mass, it is able to travel over great distances. That means the energy of our bodies, expressed as the photons emitted from our DNA, is intermingled with that of all other beings with whom our energy comes into contact. And since all DNA radiates these particles of light, it exists everywhere as a subtle energy—infusing, as it were, all of Creation.

This means that your DNA-emitted photons—the invisible part of you—cannot help but constantly interact with the invisible part of all other beings. This interaction creates yet another exciting situation. When one energy wave contacts another energy wave, it enters into a positive feedback loop. In this dynamic interaction, each element in the loop affects and is affected by the other. What this means is that, through interactions with different beings, the invisible, radiant part of you has the capacity to change and evolve. And if this information weren't staggering enough, since photons continue to travel endlessly onward, they have the ability to keep growing, interacting, and evolving, even after the body that generated them expires![5]

It seems that the long road of science is bringing us back to a more ancient understanding of the world. If we examine all this scientific information using a shamanic lens, we would call this subtle energy or vibration, *Spirit*. Perhaps, 60,000 years ago, a shaman would have understood the idea of Creation in this way: "First there is Spirit. This imperceptible force is what both shapes and infuses the body, and it is that same Spirit that radiates from us, continuing after our bodies are no longer alive."

Figure 3. Upper Paleolithic handprints are reminders of those who walked the Earth and interacted with the spirits millennia before our time.

So this view of human beings as timeless, radiant beings, interconnected to all other forms of life has parallels with cutting-edge quantum physics and pioneering genetic research; yet the people who first developed these concepts about reality lived as early as the Paleolithic era. How is it possible that these same ideas initially arose in the far-distant past? How was it possible to understand that which could not be seen, heard, or touched? It is clear that some other way of looking, listening, and feeling must have been available to them so that they could reach beyond the limitation of their senses.

For the shaman, this visionary way of perceiving the world may be an inherent outcome of the rituals necessary for attaining their powers. Shamans are initiated in ways as various as there are tribes of people on the planet, but there are parallels between many of these practices. Their common threads involve a loss or stripping away of the initiate's ordinary way of perceiving reality, as well as a detachment from the personality or ego self. This death and rebirth initiatory experience seems to be a critical aspect of shifting one's understanding of the world from focusing on matter to centering around spirit. Common threads of these ecstatic experiences include a dismemberment or dissolution of the physical body, which is followed by a gradual renewal of the flesh—sometimes appearing different or having different components than the original viscera.[6] During this experience of being dissolved or destroyed, the shamanic initiates would experience some new view of reality and their place within it. This view may show that their existence is inexorably tied to all other beings, or they may see their bodies as constructed in such a manner that they contain all living things.[7] They may describe being able to perceive light emanating from living beings[8] or experience seeing luminous threads holding the world together. These anomalous experiences of reality (*anomalous* in that they appear to defy the *reason* of Newtonian physics) are consistent with those described by people who undergo a brief period of clinical death due to severe accident, illness, or surgery.[9] It would appear that this loss of the ordinary self allows the quantum view of reality to be revealed.[10]

This loss or moving aside of the obscuring self may be accomplished in several ways. Rituals may include a form of suffering whereby a supplicant is asked to abstain from food and drink for a prescribed, lengthy period of time, or submit to extreme conditions (heat, cold, wounding) to perceive the death of self in a deep, visionary experience.[11]

When asked to define their experiences, shamans variously describe the spiritual realm as being light-filled or having sounds as its essential framework to relate the perception of a vibrational world. This is true of the shamans from the Amazon basin to the far reaches of Siberia, as well as for those contemporary individuals who have chosen to expand their perceptions beyond the ordinary.

Thankfully, it is *not* necessary for you to suffer to be a spirit walker! With a strong desire and intention, it is possible to use dancing, singing, rattling, or drumming for extended periods of time to shift out of your ordinary way of seeing the world. Indeed, repetitive auditory stimuli have the ability to create vivid visionary states that match those experienced while under the influence of sacred hallucinogens.[12] The powerful methods outlined in these pages are profoundly effective, and the information in this book will support you to make the necessary shifts in a safe way.

Perhaps It's Not Too Late
I was born into a sacred world,
Knew without the effort of instruction
That the old oak was a grandfather
And the night wind had a voice.
I knew dancing songs to celebrate the seasons
And that, if I stumbled, life would catch me.
It took much to wean me from my early ways,
Left me with blunted instincts clinging
To just pretend stories like an orphaned child.
But I have turned to return at last
Hoping against the lonely logic of long years
That life is there to catch me.

Trudy Sloan

Chapter 2

Beginning the Path

Your choice to become a spirit walker requires that you not only learn shamanic methods, but also how to be a true person of power. This path is not one of ego or grandiosity; instead, it is the humble walk into a deeper relationship with All That Is. A shaman is guided by her or his heart and celebrates the interconnections that unite and nourish all beings.

To be able to become this kind of person, you must go through an evolution. That means learning how to approach the world from a place of love and gratitude that diminishes fear and anger. This is not the tendency of the culture that surrounds you. Every day you are bathed in the energies of society's fear and anger and the painful expressions of these lower vibrations. From a widespread epidemic of anxiety and depression to outright violence and senseless mayhem, you bear witness to unconscious, poorly modulated emotional energy. In following the path of the shaman, you learn the discipline to be and behave in a more powerful way.

To start this new way of being, it is important to put yourself in an open and relaxed state of mind. The following meditation is an excellent way to center and focus yourself. It is useful not only for beginning this new venture, but also as a way to be more fully grounded and present. You may want to begin each day with it.

Read the exercise through once or twice before you begin listening to the "Embodied Light" mp3 audio file that is available for you at *www.myspiritwalk.com*.

e: Embodied Light Meditation

1. Begin by finding a quiet space where you will not be disturbed. Sit down in a comfortable chair that allows your back to be straight while your feet are on the floor.

2. With your hands folded gently in your lap, close your eyes and take a few moments to breathe. Allow your breaths to be both quiet and full—somewhat like the breaths of a deep sleep state.

3. As you begin to relax, notice that your breath originates in the center of your chest. Imagine a light there that grows brighter with every breath you take.

4. As this light grows brighter, see it also expanding to fill your entire body—growing ever brighter.

5. Your radiant body is a gift of the stars.

6. Exploding novas seeded the cosmos with all the elements to make you and the body of our beautiful planet. All the iron, calcium, oxygen, and other elements are gifts from the stars. This gift is what you inhabit while you are embodied. You are a divine radiance wrapped in star-stuff!

7. Allow your light to expand so that your physical body is enfolded in light. Your spirit—your light—completely surrounds your body. This is your true state of being.

8. Your entire being is full, rich, radiant, beautiful, and divine.

9. While continuing to breathe, notice how your radiant body is connected to the radiant body of the Earth.

10. Your body moves within the atmosphere of our planet. You live by swimming through her air with your feet touching her body. Your body is held by your light and is always cradled by the Earth.

11. Allow yourself to reach out even further and feel how the Sun's radiance embraces the Earth as she embraces you in her loving warmth. Allow all your senses to be fully enlivened by this nurturance.

12. You are an embodied light, a divine and magnificent aspect of the All That Is, made manifest by your physicality and always connected to the Earth and All That Is.

13. Breathe in the depth of this radiant, loving connection and allow it to bring you to a peaceful and fully enlivened state of being.

14. When you feel full of this experience—clasp your folded hands tightly together. As you are doing this, recall the sensations of being fully enlivened and cradled by the Earth—completely peaceful.

15. Whenever you wish, you will be able to attain this fully embodied state by repeating this symbolic gesture with your hands.

16. Now, gently release your hands and allow yourself to slowly return your attention to the room in which you are sitting. Take a full, deep, sighing breath and gently open your eyes.

Once you've read the meditation, find a comfortable position and listen to the guided version through headphones. When you feel ready, you may wish to make notes about what you experienced while doing this meditation. Take time to record all that you felt, saw, and heard.

If you experience difficulty visualizing or feeling the light at your heart center, don't worry. Sometimes it can take some time to move the consciousness down into the body and into the heart. This is especially true when we are used to being in our heads or being out of our body as a protection. Those wonderfully ingenious strategies, which may have helped us survive when we were younger, can interfere with us thriving as an adult. However, with practice you will be able to move into a heart-centered experience.

If, on the other hand, you feel foggy, confused, or light-headed after this meditation, that means you need to practice grounding yourself. Some easy ways to do this include:

- Eating a light snack
- Spending time outdoors—especially in a natural setting, with grass, trees, or by the ocean or a river
- Doing something with your hands—making something, touching stones, playing in water, or digging in dirt
- Sitting on the ground with your back up against a tree
- Breathing with a focus on the soles of your feet—feeling them touching the inside of your shoes or the ground
- Imagining roots coming from the bottom of your feet into the ground to firmly tie you to the core of the Earth
- Listening to whatever music makes you want to dance—and *dancing!*

Above all, please be gentle with yourself—especially if you find your experience with the meditation—or any other lesson in this book—feels difficult. You are in the process of transforming! This is something that is best done with a loving patience and a gentle persistence. Over time, a kind of softening begins to occur whereby the new way of being gradually becomes easier.

Choose a time of day to practice this meditation. Do this exercise with the audio file once a day for at least thirty days. As you stay with this practice, you will be able to attain this state of being more easily. Keep records of what you realize about your own process.

Process Questions

- Articulate, as best as you can, in your journal the bodily, emotional, and spiritual sensations of being simultaneously radiant and grounded on the Earth.

- How do your feelings now differ from your feelings before you practiced this meditation?

- Think about how this practice could benefit your daily life. Record your impressions.

Chapter 3

The Shaman's Paradigm of Relationship

O bservations of contemporary hunter-gatherer peoples reveal that they, like their ancestors, view the world from an
animist perspective. It seems that this "primitive" cultural
construct is intimately connected to the hunter-gatherer lifestyle.
Perhaps this stems from a need to better understand the other beings upon whom they depend for survival. When hunter-gatherers
view all of the elements of the landscape as living beings which
co-participate in the workings of life, they understand that communication with these beings is necessary for a constructive relationship. The one who is charged with the job of communicating
with these beings is the *shaman*.

The shaman's role in society is to act as a facilitator between
the human realm and that of the other spirits that inhabit the
environment. Through interaction with these spirits, shamans
understand that the intrinsic interdependencies among them all
sustain life. In addition, shamans know that we are so interconnected that we are in a constant dance of mutual impact upon one
another. Since shamanism is a historical and global phenomenon,
this worldview is a part of our collective human history.

The many spirit beings are also potential sources of power for
the shaman. This is essential, as a shaman's ability to heal is based
upon the power-filled relationships forged with the spirits.[13] Since
their shamanic abilities are dependent upon these affiliations,

shamans understand the fundamental necessity for keeping these alliances healthy and strong. An attitude of harmonious give-and-take becomes the guiding principle in exchanges within those associations. The Quechua-speaking *pacos* or shaman-healers of the high Andes refer to this idea of mutual, respectful interaction—which must be always monitored and lovingly attended to—as *ayni*, which is translated as "sacred reciprocity." By referring to this mutually beneficial interchange as *sacred*, they underline a kind of holiness to being in right relationship. In other words, when we interact in this manner, we are somehow more in alignment with the fundamental framework of existence.

As a spirit walker, the relationships you forge with the spirits of the natural world can provide comfort, a sense of peace, a feeling of oneness, and strength that can be attained no other way. In effect, you develop a sense of "being home" wherever you are on the planet. This reconnection with the spirits of the Earth also provides you with supportive energy. It is the kind of energy that will help you to move through life with more joy, clarity, and purpose.

Just like members of a hunter-gatherer society, we are surrounded with other beings with which we need to communicate in order to create a mutually beneficial situation. The spirits, too, need to be in relationship with people. Compassionate, healing spirits are committed to providing their guidance and support toward creating a healthy and balanced world. However, in spite of their great wisdom and "big picture" perspective, they are unable to physically impact this Earthly reality because they are not themselves physical beings. When we enter into partnerships with these compassionate spirits, we contribute our own physicality and, as their intermediaries, become true cocreators. It is this blending of powers—the nonphysical power of the spirits and physical powers of the shamans' heartfelt interactions with them—that has the greatest potential for manifesting true miracles.[14]

So how do we reenter the way of being that allows us to work with the spirits who surround us? The answer is learning how to be in *reverent participatory relationship* with all beings. The word *reverent* implies feeling and expressing a profound respect or veneration as well as a willingness to show consideration or appreciation. *Participatory* means that we take an active part in the relationship.

Consulting physician for the Glasgow Homeopathic Hospital and renowned medical conference speaker David Reilly, MD, has proven that an effective therapeutic encounter—that is, one where a healing response has been engendered—is based in such relationships. Dr. Reilly suggests that "traditional and indigenous healing systems including shamanism have spent a long time learning about these things—translating it to our world is the challenge." In regard to our own bodies' capacity to heal, Dr. Reilly notes, "We know a human recovery reaction is a built in potential, we have seen that it can be modified for good and bad by *human interaction*."[15] Dr. Reilly teaches that being considerate and respectful—and really listening to the patient—can in fact become a primary healing modality. In his presentations, he offers case histories with videos of patient encounters, which consistently prove the efficacy of his method. Simply by listening deeply and respectfully to a patient and asking compassionate questions about what he has heard, he has been able to resolve many of the hospital's most challenging patient cases.

I believe we are all hardwired for this level of interaction. If it were not so, it would not have such a powerful effect upon our bodies, minds, and spirits.

Maintaining a reverent attitude in all interactions is, in and of itself, a challenge when we consider the society in which we currently live. With the exclusion of those who follow a more holistic worldview, we as a society do not generally respect one another's opinions and perspectives. Nor do we see our fundamental interdependencies with nature and with each other upon which we depend for our survival. Furthermore, our societal perspectives on relationship are skewed by unhealthy ways of relating such as power abuse or codependency. As a result, a supportive framework needs to be put in place to both facilitate and encourage interactions that are focused toward reverence and participation. It is clear to me that if we want to reshape our current human culture into one that's more ecologically sound, we can start by making *reverent participatory relationship* our guiding principle.

An experience I had a few years back showed me that thoughtfulness toward another may be innate. I was in British Columbia, watching a mother grizzly bear and her two cubs making their way along the bank of the Atnarko River during the annual salmon run. Mother bear, in the lead, was moving briskly along through the brush with her cubs straggling behind. The siblings were separated from each other by several yards. At a bend in the river, the mother bear made her way out of the vegetation and onto the graveled shore.

A few moments later, the first cub arrived at that same bend in the river. It looked down the river at its retreating mother and then back toward its sibling who was still in the thicket. It checked back and forth several times and then did something amazing. While one can imagine that it would have been more biologically advantageous to run along and be the only cub for the mother bear to care for, the first bear cub simply sat down and waited. When its sibling finally caught up, the two of them scampered down the bank after their mother. It was clear to me at that moment that the act of considering another being is not unique to human beings, but rather an intrinsic part of the beautifully elaborate dance of life.

Reverent Participatory Relationship within Your Self

In following the path of the spirit walker, you have chosen to become more conscious than many people surrounding you. While others may act unconsciously, your vocation demands that you learn to behave in a manner that is consistently more balanced and whole. To accomplish this, it is necessary to accept responsibility for your reactions and then root out those places in the self that cause turbulent or dissonant responses to arise. It is a journey toward living each moment with focus and intentionality.

As Nepalese shaman Bhola Nath Banstola has said,

> The shaman's relationship with the spirits and the sacred depends upon the personal relationship they have with themselves. If they have a very deep relationship with themselves, high awareness, an open heart, deep confidence in what they do, and a belief in themselves, then their relationship with the outside world will be always harmonious. This strong inner confidence and harmonious relationship with the outer world help a shaman to create a fluid relationship with the spirits—a good relationship with the spiritual world.

Shamans have understood for millennia that we cocreate ⌣. reality through our thoughts and feelings. Creation is not a singular act, but rather a continuous process. Unconscious, unfocused, and unintentional thoughts and feelings create needless suffering, discord, and discomfort in your life. On the other hand, when you become more conscious and learn the way of mastering the inner technology of your feelings, you can begin to generate a life of harmony, peace, and healing. This is the vibration that is most effective, and it is the one with which powerful shamans strive to align themselves. You can think about it as the *original vibration*. By that I mean that it is the energetic framework that continues to create and evolve the natural world. Since we are an inexorable part of the natural world, we change continually, and through the powerful forces of our feelings, we also contribute to change. At every moment, whether we are conscious of it or not, we are affecting the health and well-being of All That Is.

While the dissonant energies of unconscious humans are powerful, they do not create. Instead, they cause disruptions that interfere with the natural flow of life-giving forces. When human beings choose to become conscious and stop disrupting the flow of creation, a field of harmonious energy radiates from them. This produces an environment that is more conducive to healing and balance. In essence, you make the leap to becoming a conscious cocreator!

Exercise: Identifying a Single Day's Worth of Interconnections

Using your journal, start listing every being with whom you interact in one day. Start with the face-to-face connections at home and at work and include all the nonhumans as well. When you are through with this more obvious list, begin adding all the beings that were not visible but with whom your life was connected.

For instance, if you bought a cup of coffee, you would list the barista and cashier and then think about the people who raised, picked, transported, and roasted the beans. Then add the plants that grew the beans. To this, add the place in which the plant was nurtured. Then list the spirits of wind, water, sun, and soil that nurture those plants. Think next about how the beans were transported to your coffee shop. Did they make a journey across an ocean? Imagine that trip and estimate all the beings there that were a part of the journey. Think next about the cup. Is it paper? Who were the trees that became that paper? What land nurtured them? If the cup is pottery, think about the clay soil that was transformed by the same element of fire that roasted the beans for your coffee.

Take this exercise as deeply as you can so that you accumulate in your notebook all the interdependencies that helped to make your day possible. When your day is done, breathe quietly and give thanks for all of the beings that have touched your life.

Process Questions

- Articulate, as best as you can, in your journal the bodily, emotional, and spiritual sensations of recognizing the breadth and depth of your interconnectedness.

- How does your view of your world differ from the way you felt before this exercise? Record what you notice.

Chapter 4

The Creative Power of Emotions

O ver the millennia, shamans have gained mastery over the invisible world. Our emotional energy is a part of this invisible world. Feelings impact our reality as powerfully as any spirit does. Indeed, our feelings affect the very same sphere of reality—beyond linear time and space—that a shaman would refer to as "the spirit world."

Our feelings affect each other's health and well-being. For instance, when someone around us is in a bad mood, it can very quickly become contagious. This kind of energy may even contribute to illness. "The shamanic perception of well being . . . depend(s) on ideas of balance, flow and equilibrium in the environment, and on ideas of giving and withholding, love and anger, and motivation and intention among the spirits which animate this environment."[16] In learning how our emotional energies impact our bodies and the world around us, we can begin to bring another level of consciousness to all of our interactions.

It is important to clarify the terms *emotion* and *feeling*, as they are related but different. Emotions are pure information we receive from the physical world. They are simple in nature—mad, sad, glad, scared. Feelings, however, are what happen when our minds respond to the input we have received through our emotions. Our minds, seeking to find order in the chaos of emotion, add their own input in the form of thoughts shaded by previous experience. This blend of emotion plus thought produces feelings as a response to the situation. These feelings then cascade energetic and biochemical messages throughout and beyond the body.

There are several key points that are important to know about feelings and their impact on our ordinary, daily reality.

You Are a Being of Vibration

Physicist Mark Comings, PhD, has been involved in exploring the foundations of physics through a number of innovative, elegant, and unconventional conceptual approaches. His focus has been on the physics of space, time, light, and energy. At the 2005 True North annual medical conference, Comings shared some of the exciting information that is being taught in the New Physics. Fundamental to this new view is an understanding that matter—the stuff of our physical reality—isn't solid at all. In fact, everything is vibration.[17] All matter—our bodies, the elements, and everything that exists in our physical world—is first and foremost vibration. This vibration is the invisible part of us that a tribal shaman would call spirit.

Your Feelings Are Energetic Information

According to Comings, more recent scientific viewpoints also consider human consciousness to be an intrinsic feature of the field of reality and a central feature of both physics and biology.[18] Consciousness is an amalgamation of our thoughts and our feelings. According to the New Physics, it is responsible for actually creating the reality we experience as physical! In addition, our feelings are the more powerful aspect of our consciousness, as they have the greatest impact upon the nature of reality.

Indeed, in the lecture mentioned above, Dr. Comings spoke at length about how all reality is a part of a fabric of light (vibration) and that matter is initially a standing wave pattern in that light. He further added that it is our feelings that have the power to "crystallize" the light from a wave or vibration into a tangible physicality.

Your Feelings Alter DNA—Yours and That of Others

Experiments by the Institute of HeartMath have been used to observe the molecular building blocks of the body, our DNA. These observations, applying an ultraviolet absorption spectrophotometer, have shown that the physical conformation of DNA is directly affected by our emotional energy. When stressed by angry, fearful, or anxious emotions, our DNA twists tightly onto itself forming what I refer to as a "DNA cramp." This is important because the shape of the DNA strand determines how effectively the DNA regulatory processes function. The conformational states of the DNA molecule are important in DNA replication and repair as well as the creation of proteins and enzymes that regulate a wide variety of basic cell functions. The tighter the cramp, the less effective our DNA becomes at accomplishing necessary duties.

This overall loss of function due to a DNA cramp also plays out in our brains. When stressed by DNA cramping, your body produces different hormones than during periods of inner harmony. These biochemicals, such as adrenaline and cortisol, flood your body and have the effect of chemically denying you access to the upper, reasoning functions of your brain and increasing access to the lower, fight/flight/freeze mechanism. As anyone who has drawn a blank while trying to answer a simple question in a stressful situation can attest, this cramp limits one's ability to respond effectively. You and I are simply not at our best or fullest capacity when we are angry or afraid.

While we can feel these changes in our own bodies, the researchers also found that experiencing anxiety, fear, or anger created biological changes not only *within* the individual, *but outside of the body as well.* The Institute of HeartMath placed samples of the donor's DNA in two different laboratories that were separated by a half a mile. Each sample was monitored with the identical equipment.[19] In one of the laboratories, a test subject adept at recalling her feelings held one of the donor DNA samples. When that person brought up feelings of compassion and gratitude, the samples in *both* laboratories relaxed into perfect conformation. On the other hand, when the test subject felt angry or anxious, both test samples wound into a DNA cramp. What was even more amazing was that both of the DNA samples reacted simultaneously.

Why did this happen? The feeling energies transmitted by our bodies are quantum and nonlocal in nature. That is, they not only exist in a point of time and space—our body—they also exist beyond the limits of time and space—the infinite. Amazingly, laboratory experiments have measured effects of transmitted feelings over half a mile from their generating source, and the effects were instantaneous.[20] There was no time lag.

Studies by Glen Rein, PhD, and Rollin McCraty, PhD, determined that the strongest "energy generator" in our bodies—that is the source of the strongest magnetic and electrical fields—is our heart.[21] Our heart is what pulses the energy of our feelings into the world. Since all living beings—animals, birds, fish, plants, and trees—have DNA, our feelings are having a constant impact on the foundations of creation and on life's continuance.

Loving Feelings Produce Harmony

When we experience deep feelings of love, compassion, or appreciation, we radiate coherent frequencies throughout our bodies, promoting health and vitality. These feelings have the capacity to bring your DNA into its most harmonious state of being. This state is consistent with improved immune and cellular function—that is, optimum health. In addition, since the immune system and related hormonal systems directly impact your brain function, these coherent energies improve your ability to think more clearly.

Our harmonious feelings provide us with a direct way to align ourselves with what Comings refers to as the multidimensional "sea of radiance" which unites everything. When we align ourselves in such a manner, we are remembering what has always been so. Nothing can be outside of everything—we are a part of All That Is. During this aligning and remembering, we shift our vibration so that it is healing both for ourselves and the creatures that surround us. When we shift our feeling states and thus our vibration, we create profound and measurable changes. Science is providing a clear understanding of how this works.

Dissonant Feelings Create Disruption

When "negative" feelings cause DNA to wind tightly onto itself, the DNA's ability to regulate cellular function or repair and replicate itself is impaired. This condition interferes with the health of the organism.

Laboratory analyses measuring the levels of SIgA (Salivary Immunoglobulin A), which is an easy-to-measure immune system indicator, have proven that a ten-minute expression of anger produces a six-hour decline in a test subject's immune response. On the other hand, when a ten-minute period of compassion, love, or gratitude is felt, there is a measurable six-hour boost in the immune system.

Shockingly, this interference impacts all other beings around us as well. In the Rein/McCraty studies, all subjects capable of generating strong loving feelings could alter the conformation of DNA *according to their intention.* The intention to unwind or wind the DNA produced corresponding increases or decreases in the UV absorption peak, which indicated alterations in the physical/chemical structure of one or more of the bases in the DNA molecule. That is to say, these subjects made actual changes in the DNA structure itself. Untrained individuals, who were not able to sustain feelings of love, showed low ratios of ECG coherence and were unable to intentionally alter the conformation of DNA.

Conversely, one individual in the study was upset and frustrated—having little control over his emotions. This individual showed an unusually low ECG coherence ratio. However because of the strong intensity of his emotional experience, his energy caused an increased winding of the DNA and a negative change in the genetic material being observed. Although the incoherent energy associated with frustration resulted in a change in DNA, this individual could not intentionally bring about this change.

The frustrated test subject was experiencing a DNA cramp. Importantly, even though this subject could cramp the DNA, he couldn't relax it—no matter what his intention—while experiencing these incoherent feelings. On the other hand, the persons who were experiencing the loving feelings *could* relax the DNA—even the DNA that was twisted onto itself by the feelings of the frustrated subject!

Not All Negative Feelings Are Fully Conscious

Part of our work as a shaman is to recognize unconscious impediments and negative beliefs that are impacting our reality and our physical bodies. Like inner saboteurs, these feelings can undermine our best conscious efforts to transform our lives and change.

In 2007, my partner and I gave the keynote presentation, "The Creative Power of Emotions" at the health care conference, "Out of the Ordinary—Possibilities in Health," in Austin, Texas. There we met fellow presenter, Harold "Hal" Robinson, a counselor who has integrated modern psychotherapeutic practices with the traditional Native American ceremony of the Enemy Way. While the traditional, Diné (Navajo) Enemy Way Ceremony is used to restore a warrior's spiritual health after battle, Robinson uses this language to describe the act of tracking down our unconscious patterns of belief and unhealthy perceptions that interfere with our mental and emotional well-being.

He gave a wonderful example of this work in action: He described his wife as a person of intelligence whom he respected. One day, however, he found that he was upset and frustrated by her behavior. As we all do, he became angry—thinking to himself, "Stupid woman!"—and so hurried himself into the car and off to work. On the way, he found he was being frustrated and angry with the driver of another car who was also female. "Ah, another stupid woman!" he thought. This pattern continued at work with his usually very intelligent coworker. It was at that point that it finally dawned on him that the pattern that was frustrating him didn't exist outside his mind. He was not really surrounded by "stupid women." Instead, he realized that this particular morning, his wife had triggered something from his unconscious that was a reaction to a circumstance he experienced in his childhood in relationship with his mother. He went home and apologized to his wife. He thanked her for revealing another "enemy" inside of himself and for helping him to realize that he had more inner work to do!

Robinson believes that performing the work of the spiritual warrior requires humility, courage, and tenacity. I would argue that it is also our first task on the way to becoming a good shaman. One cannot presume to understand the workings of the Universe or desire to dance with the elemental powers without first embracing the present moment and facing each challenge as a test of spirit. By doing so, you strengthen and supplement your understanding of yourself. Since each of us exists as a microcosm of the larger world, this also helps us to better understand All That Is.

As you uncover your inner "enemies"—which are actually your allies in helping you to clear out limiting patterns and beliefs—get the support you need to release them in a healthy way. Along with your gratitude practice, seek the company of a supportive professional such as a counselor to assist you in this work of clearing. This is important, as none of us received these unbeneficial beliefs in a vacuum. We got them through family relationships, other close associations, and our cultural values. It is for this reason that stepping into a therapeutic relationship can not only heal conscious beliefs and patterns but also reveal unconscious beliefs. In this way you can more quickly release yourself from suffering and accelerate your magnificent transformation. This is especially important as a spirit walker recognizes that what happens on the inside has an impact on others, and vice versa.

Mastery of Feelings Is an Essential Skill

When you choose to generate coherent feelings of love, gratitude, appreciation, or compassion, you produce healing effects not only within your own body but also throughout the DNA-filled ecosystem.

I am not suggesting that you learn to suppress your feelings, but rather that you understand how to work with them for the most benefit. Just as nerves in our hands signal to us if a surface is too hot to touch, our emotions give us clues about our environment. We must experience our emotions so we may understand the clues they are giving us about a situation. However, the point where we can alter our responses is the place where the emotion meets the mind. At this junction, we can consciously choose how we wish to respond to a situation—thereby developing mastery of our inner technology. While the input we receive is not solely under our influence, changing our perceptions is. We can alter the learned reactions that are embedded in our minds and personalities and thus our consciousness. Through changing our perceptions and consequently changing our reactions, we shift the vibrations we put into the world. In this way, we become conscious creators, *consciously* affecting what physicists refer to as the quantum plenum. The quantum plenum is simply the *playing field of infinite, superimposed possibilities.*

Because our feelings have such a profound effect on both the inner and outer physical worlds, spirit walkers have a responsibility to develop mastery of their feelings for the benefit of their own health and the world's well-being. By fostering feelings of love, compassion, appreciation, and gratitude, you can provide yourself—and all other creatures—an antidote to the damaging effects of fear and anger. For instance, by nurturing compassion you will be more able to *feel* your interconnections with other beings. This feeling of interconnectedness can move you to find ways to alleviate suffering. And it is not only the family of human beings that experiences suffering in this moment; every creature on our planet is caught in the tightening net of global climate change and environmental degradation. It's clear that our family—from our human family to the larger one that includes all beings—is in dire need of support.

The late Stephen Jay Gould, an influential evolutionary biologist at Harvard, once said, "We cannot win this battle to save species and environments without forging an emotional bond between ourselves and nature as well—for we will not fight to save what we do not love." If we're honest with ourselves, we realize that we do only conserve what we love, and at the most basic level most of us love ourselves, our family, our friends, and our community beyond in expanding concentric circles. As we go further out from the center, there is usually a weakening urgency and commitment. However, as a shaman, you will need to develop an understanding that embraces your larger family with the same heart you lavish on your immediate circle. All of us depend on our larger family for our survival—we suffer as they suffer, we become unhealthy as they become unhealthy. It is a true and basic connection that you and I cannot live without.

From this moment forward, you can no longer afford the luxury of wallowing in negative feeling states. Fear, anger, and frustration negatively impact your body and the bodies of all other beings. At this time on the planet, there is no more dramatic action you can take in the world than to learn to work with your feeling energies.

Your Feelings Are a Primary Tool for Transformation

When you develop a practice of feeling gratitude, you begin to consciously access your Creator Self. Developing a practice of gratitude can begin very simply. Take a moment each day to remember a situation when you felt grateful. Recall the feelings that you experienced at that time and let them fill you up again. Give yourself the time to feel really full. Now imagine that these feelings filling you up have nowhere else to go but to radiate out of your body with every one of your heartbeats. You remain full even as this vibration of gratitude is being broadcast from your body. As you experience this, add an intention that you wish to manifest. Do not worry about details, but rather put out the feelings that you wish to experience. By this I mean do not put out that you *want* something—a new partner, a new job, etc.—but rather *how it feels to have it*. By feeling it already accomplished, you are engaging in its actual creation.

When you blend conscious intention with feelings of gratitude or appreciation, the intention is much more likely to manifest. This amazing process has been proven by Dr. Emoto in his experiments with water, and by Sandra Ingerman in her *Medicine for the Earth* work. While being observed by scientists, a small, harmonious group of people feeling gratitude and holding strong intentions have "healed" covered beakers of water that had been intentionally polluted with ammonium hydroxide. This pollutant, which arises from both human and animal waste, is a common contaminant of groundwater. It causes problems in the environment in two ways: First, it literally poisons the water. Second, it has the ability to make oil-based pollutants such as PCBs, gasoline, and benzene water soluble, thereby making them more easily absorbed by plants, animals, and human beings.

Through no other means but the power of feeling-based ceremonies, conducted in an atmosphere of reverence for the Earth, the polluted water changed from a poisonous pH level of 11.5 to one of a nearly drinkable pH of 9. This shift of over two points of pH is the equivalent of a thousand-fold change and was accomplished in a ceremony that lasted less than an hour. The impossibly swift change seen in these ceremonies is truly unexplainable by scientific means.

As David R. Hawkins writes in *Power vs. Force*, "Every thought, action, decision, or feeling creates an eddy in the interlocking, interbalancing, ever-moving energy fields of life, leaving a permanent record for all time."[22] So no matter what language we use to refer to the fabric of All That Is, it is now clear that our beliefs and our feelings actually program that fabric, creating our reality. Up until now, we have been creating unconsciously. Feelings coupled with our intentions and subsequent actions shape the very physical essence of our reality. There is no longer any doubt that we are creator beings. As we learn to be conscious—as well as compassionate—we take our next evolutionary leap as a species.

Exercise: Working with Fear and Anger—
Releasing a "DNA Cramp"

Experiencing anger or fear is a natural reaction. It is also true that these feelings create disruption. We cannot simply suppress "negative" feelings, as unexpressed feelings are like a festering wound that continues to poison the body. In addition, when feelings are suppressed, we cannot harvest the information they are trying to provide. This may be more information about our situation or clues about the old wounds that we still carry. Learning how to receive the information our emotional body gives us and then release the disruptive feelings is a critical part of becoming a healthy and powerful spirit walker. Relieving a DNA cramp is an important step in developing mastery of your feelings and a first step in creative manifestation.

Read through the exercise once or twice before you begin listening to the guided mp3 audio file that is available for you at *www.myspiritwalk.com* so you can gather the memories that you will need to recall during the exercise.

1. Be still and begin breathing with a focus on your heart—as though your breaths originate in the center of your chest. Breathe for at least 10–15 breaths or until you feel yourself beginning to relax.

2. While continuing to breathe, remember a time when you felt grateful. It can be a feeling memory from the recent or distant past.

3. Allow yourself to fill with the feelings of that remembered moment.

4. Once you really feel full of gratitude, allow those feelings to radiate from your body with each of your heartbeats.

Listen to this guided meditation and practice it at least twice daily, since developing emotional intelligence is necessary for becoming an effective shamanic practitioner. Practice until you can easily shift out of "negative emotions" anyplace and in any situation. I cannot stress enough how critically important this ability is to becoming a true hea... force!

As you continue to practice this daily, keep a journal of what you realize about your own process. This is important, as self-knowledge is one of the keys to being a powerful shaman. Indeed, the mastery of our emotions is a crucial part of coming into harmony with the larger Harmony which we refer to as Divine and, therefore, critical for creating a new and beautiful model of life for yourself and your world.

Process Questions

- Honestly ask yourself in what situations are you triggered into anger.

- What are your underlying fears? When do you believe that they began?

- Think about how having emotional "mastery" could benefit your daily life. Record all that you discover.

Chapter 5

Gratitude in Action: Making Shaman Prayers

B y creating a baseline of gratitude and working through your old limiting beliefs, you begin to unleash your creative energies. These energies are combined and aligned with the power that surrounds all of us in the natural world. They are then focused by the supportive guidance from helpful and compassionate spirits, giving a spirit walker her or his abilities to help and heal.

Once you have identified your old outmoded perceptions and troublesome feelings from the past, you can begin to envision your new self and new life. This is a powerful step in changing your reality and an important tool in your shamanic practice. Once you are feeling really full of gratitude, use your brilliant imagination to create a scenario that produces feelings of your desire being already fulfilled. Remember, the imagery you bring to mind is whatever you need to generate the feelings. It is your feelings that become your tool for manifestation. Feelings are the prayer!

For example, if you feel that you don't have enough, you would imagine ways in which you feel that you have *more* than enough. You may imagine being able to effortlessly provide for your family's needs. You may imagine yourself sitting with a loved one in a beautiful place feeling perfectly at ease. Simple affirmations often fail because the underlying feelings haven't changed. By transforming your feelings, you actually begin transforming your reality. Once you have had this change of heart and mind, you will find that your efforts toward your goal feel more supported. You may see opportunities that you never saw before or draw more like-minded individuals to your inner circle. These shifts are made possible by your change of mind/heart and the energetic signature that they produce in and around your body.

One more thing, remember to feel what you desire happening now—not in some future time. If you feel it as something in the future, it will remain in the future. It means feeling that you are fulfilled in this present moment, not feeling that you will be satisfied someday. Brother David Steindl-Rast[23] states, "In daily life we must see that it is not happiness that makes us grateful, but gratefulness that makes us happy." By living in gratitude, we help create the very situations we desire to experience. This happens because all matter initially exists as a wave or vibration that *may* take form. Physical expression happens when the wave is collapsed into a point in time and space. By consciously working with the inner technology of our feelings, we can change the wave or vibratory state that in turn changes the nature of reality. In a sense, our feelings decide how the waves collapse into physicality.

Indeed, Dr. David R. Hawkins, MD, PhD, an internationally renowned psychiatrist, physician, researcher, and pioneer in the fields of consciousness research and spirituality, wrote in his book *Power vs. Force*, "We all float on the collective level of consciousness of (hu)man kind, so that any increment we add comes back to us."[24] Plainly put, that means, if you project fear, you'll be bathing in more fear, and if you radiate gratitude and love, you'll actually produce more to be grateful for! This state enables you to feel lighter, be more compassionate, and more easily radiate healing energy into the world.

In addition, try not to get locked into the idea that there is only one way of fulfilling your dreams. The spirits of All That Is may have something in mind even more glorious than you can imagine, so always focus on simply feeling it in this present moment. That is the ticket to weaving your new way of being. More importantly, you will already be having the feelings that you desire most in your life. Having felt them richly every day, you will sustain the courage to keep going forward and weave them more and more into reality.

~~~~~~

Exercise: Prayer from the Heart

This process begins in the same fashion that relieving a "DNA cramp" begins. Read through it once or twice before you begin listening to the guided mp3 audio file available on *www.myspiritwalk.com*.

1. Start breathing with a focus on your heart—as though your breaths originate in the center of your chest. Breathe for at least 10–15 breaths or until you relax.

2. While you continue to breathe, remember a time when you felt grateful. It can be a feeling memory from the recent or distant past.

3. Allow yourself to fill with the feelings of that remembered moment.

4. As you really feel full of gratitude, allow those feelings to radiate from your body with each of your heartbeats.

5. Once you feel truly full and feel your gratitude radiating out from your heart, let yourself imagine your prayers already fulfilled. Allow this new feeling to ride on the gratitude radiating out from your body into the world. Use your splendid imagination to provide a complete feeling picture of the desired outcome. Use all of your senses, but do not limit your picture with specific scenarios. Focus on the way you desire to feel. Your prayers are no more or less important than anyone else's, so it is especially important to include the benefit your prayers have upon All That Is!

Practice this meditation often. You are transforming the matrix of energy to manifest your desired feeling outcome. Do not despair if you don't see immediate results. Transforming your old, outmoded ways of perceiving the world takes time and patience. Be persistent and continue working with gratitude in your life.

Process Questions

- Were you able to imagine with feeling?

- Was one of your senses more powerful in eliciting stronger feelings? Make a record of what you discovered about your senses.

- Did negative feelings intrude upon your process? If so, what were they? Write them down and see if you can get in touch with their source inside of you.

- As you continue to practice this daily, keep records of what you realize about your own process.

Since gratitude (love, appreciation, and compassion) has such power, it is essential to develop a strong practice of gratitude. Gratitude needs to become your baseline feeling. The actions that you take in your day can strengthen it so that it becomes easier and easier to step back into the feeling. This creates a change in your fundamental makeup on a mental, emotional, and even physiological level.

Making shaman prayers can accelerate this transformation and, in the process, bring a great deal more joy and pleasure to your experience of life. You can think of it as a win-win-win scenario. The world around you benefits from your feelings of gratitude at the same time you feel better inside and better about your world!

Making Daily Offerings

As a part of our spiritual practice, my partner and I make frequent offerings in nature. These rituals have become part of the fabric of our days and another way for us to show gratitude. When I share with people that we do this, many people feel overwhelmed at the thought of adding something to their busy schedule. Yet, the act of offering our gratitude actually smoothes the path for our day and helps us to reset when we find ourselves slipping into a limiting thought or feeling.

Your gratitude offering rituals do not always have to be complicated. This is especially true of ones you can easily perform daily. These can be very simple, indeed. Here is an example that entails feeding the spirits in an atmosphere of gratitude.

Exercise: Shaman Prayers—Making an Offering

1. First, choose something you want to "feed" the spirits. Use something that is readily available and gentle on the Earth and her creatures.[25] Asian shamans use many different kinds of offerings including blessed water, milk, candy, flowers, fruits, multicolored strips of cloths, and grains. While Native Americans of the American Southwest use a small pinch of corn pollen, you may want to

choose something like cornmeal or another flour, dried flower petals, or birdseed. Make it something that you find easy to carry with
you at all times. You may want to make a special pouch for your
offering material.[26]

2. Choose a place/time that makes sense to you for your offering.
Remember this doesn't have to be complicated! You can set out an
offering before you go out your door each day, you can step outside for a bit while your coffee perks or feed the spirits just before
you get into your car.

3. It is imperative to enter into feeling gratitude before you make your
offering. This emotional content is the actual prayer. The action
of making an offering helps you to remember and produce the
feeling. The ritual helps you to remember that you are in a constant state of "giving" into the fabric of All That Is. When we are
in gratitude we are giving the vibrations of health, well-being, and
abundance in all their beneficial forms into the quantum plenum
for manifestation.

4. When you feel completely full of gratitude, give thanks for your life
with a small offering from the heart. Take a pinch of whatever safe
substance you have chosen to use and place it on the land or into
the water or up into the air with reverence.

5. Consciously breathe in with gratitude and breathe it out again.
Then go about your day.

Process Questions

- What did you feel as you made your gratitude offering to the spirits?

- How did your sensations (hearing, sight, touch, sense of smell) shift
as you made your gratitude offering?

- What are the times of day that you will choose to make a simple
offering?

- Why do those points in your day feel important to you? Record your impressions.

- Think about how making these offerings contributes to your experience of daily life.

- As you continue to practice this daily, keep records of what you realize about your own process.

The simple offering ritual outlined above may be accomplished in a few moments. Even though it is so easy, a daily practice such as this can deeply transform your experience of life. You may wish to make more than one offering in your day. Whenever I feel bogged down on a project or out of sorts, I go outside for another gratitude offering. This humble ritual shifts me in a more positive direction.

Chapter 6

Shamanic Imagination and the Science of Manifestation

I
t has been said that no change is possible without being able to imagine it first. Since the changes we are participating in have never previously existed on the Earth, it becomes necessary to have a tool by which we can have experiences of new possibilities. Igniting our imagination allows us to access the feelings of the new possibilities, apply them in our feeling prayers, and finally manifest them. If we desire to create a new reality for ourselves, our entire species, and the planet as a whole, we need to be able to find that access to the new reality *before* it has manifested!

Indeed, to actually create the new reality, we need to *feel* that which we haven't yet experienced. To be able to feel that which is hidden from us by time or distance, we need to have a tool that can take us beyond our current experience of reality. We need to be able to enter the place that science calls the nonlocal universe—the invisible realms of the spirits.

Connecting with the Invisible Realms

To be a spirit walker, you must be able to function in both the local and nonlocal universe—the visible and invisible worlds. One way spirit walkers enter the invisible realms is through the shamanic journey. Since human perceptions about the nature of the world—

what we understand as ordinary reality—are primarily based on the information provided by our senses, other ways of perceiving must be called upon to gain information about the unseen world. The shamanic journey offers the opportunity to intentionally expand our perceptions outside of ordinary time and space for the specific purpose of gaining information, insight, or experiences that are normally hidden from us. The usually imperceptible light energies that comprise creation become palpable to spirit walkers when they attain an altered state of consciousness. In other words, in this state, we are able to perceive the world of <u>vibration</u> that is constantly in the process of creating ordinary reality.

This way to access the invisible realms has stood the test of time and may indeed be as old as human culture itself. The framework for the shamanic journey has its roots in hunter-gatherer culture. Peoples following this lifestyle lived in small groups and slept in temporary camps. Each morning, the entire group would embark upon the work of the day which included gathering the necessities for life: food, firewood, plant material to make nets, pads for sleeping, etc. Once the day's work was complete, the entire band would again return to the central camp to share in the bounty and prepare what was gathered.

For much of the time, the usual human abilities of vision, hearing, toolmaking, and mobility were enough to bring resolution to the problems of daily survival. However, sometimes a need arose that was not as easily met by ordinary means. For instance, if several members of the tribal group fell ill, this would significantly impact the survival potential of the whole since each member was called upon to provide for the group. Yet, <u>why they were ill</u> and how they could be made well were not something that could be known by using ordinary methods. What plants could effect a cure and where did they grow? Another example might be the location of herd animals or migrating flocks when they were not in the local range. How might a band of human beings who traveled on foot be able to know in which direction to travel?

To solve these essential riddles of survival, a member of the band needed to be able to expand her or his ordinary awareness to include that which was usually unseen, unheard, or untouched. The individual needed to embark from the camp in a different way using spiritual eyes and ears to find that which was as necessary as the gathering of food. Such individuals came to be known as *shamans*, and their *shamanic journeys* evolved as a necessary concrete, problem-solving tool.

Traditional shamans believe that the spirit of any individual is capable of taking flight; that is, the spirit may partially leave the body.[27] This leaving and returning of the spirit is done intentionally by the shaman, for purposes of looking beyond our ordinary time and space reality.[28] Many cultures utilized some form of repetitive sound to expand awareness, and the drum is common to many different shamanic traditions. Although shamanic trances were sometimes induced through magical plants, repetitive drumming is very effective in bringing on and sustaining an expanded, shamanic state of consciousness.

Entering this altered state of consciousness makes transcending of barriers of the known world possible. It is the shamanic journey and the act of leaving ordinary time and space—"walking between the worlds"—that separates the work of a shaman from other kinds of spiritual traditions.

When shamans enter the spirit world, they interact with their spirit helpers. These nonphysical beings exist beyond the physical world and are a source of healing, guidance, and wisdom. To be effective, a shaman has to develop a relationship with these beings. The shaman's spirit helpers function as companions, wise teachers, and interpreters of that which is as yet unknown to the shaman. They help the shaman to comprehend what lies beyond ordinary human understanding.

While shamanism and journeying may have their roots in our past and our need to survive, using these methods today can help you to transform your reality and *thrive*—not only as an individual but also as part of an intact biosphere. The tool of journeying can open your mind and heart to unimagined possibilities and give you experiences of them that you can feel. With that access, you can weave a future that is rich with healing, harmony, and wonder.

Exercise: Engaging Your Non-Ordinary Awareness

To prepare yourself for entering the world of spirit, it is useful to explore what senses are engaged while imagining and to give them some exercise. You are going to imagine yourself on a visit to the planet Mars! This exercise is a useful way to stretch your mind's ability to deal with information that isn't based in the ordinary perception of reality.

1. Begin this exercise by getting comfortably seated, closing your eyes, and practicing the Embodied Light meditation.

2. Once you have completed the meditation, begin imagining your trip to Mars. Perceive the details of this experience as richly as you are able—with sight, sound, touch, smell, and your feelings.

3. Do this for about twenty minutes, and then bring yourself back to Earth and the room in which you are sitting.

4. Once you are settled on terra firma, take out your journal and record all of the details of how you function when stepping outside of your everyday way of being.

While you were on this imaginary voyage to another planet, notice which of your ways of perceiving was typically the strongest. Were you seeing the scene? Did you get a sense of textures or sounds? Did you have emotional feelings while you were engaged in the process? Did it make you nervous, excited, exhilarated? Notice too, if your mind kept interrupting the process with distracting thoughts. Oftentimes, the mind needs to learn to trust unusual experiences more fully to allow you to stretch even more into the unseen realms. Coupling the Embodied Light meditation with this imaginary voyaging is a way to assist the mind in exploring new realities beyond the ordinary.

Process Questions

Take a few moments to ask yourself these questions about your desire to undertake journeying between the worlds.

- Why do you desire a deeper connection to All That Is?

- What is your deeper purpose for seeking higher guidance and insight?

- What questions do you have that haven't been answered by ordinary means?

- Record what you have realized about your own desires.

Uroboros
If imaginary beings aren't real
Then imagination is.
But if imaginary beings are real
Then imagination doesn't exist.
Difficult, yes, but if
You seek to understand,
Resist the urge to simplify,
To separate the mirror from its image.
For if you scrape silver imagination
Off the clear glass of reality
You may never see yourself again.

TRUDY SLOAN

Chapter 7

Shamanic Journeying

The shamanic journey provides us with a doorway to the Invisible World—the Worlds of Spirit that are beyond our knowing which exist outside of or beyond our understanding of time and space. The actual word *spirit* comes down to us from the Latin root "spirare"[29] which means *to breathe*. Even though this work may seem new to you, with practice it can become as easy as breathing!

East of the Sun and West of the Moon: The Worlds of the Spirits

Around the globe, the spirit world is described as a place. This is a way we humans translate the numinous world of the spirit into something within which we can move by shifting our awareness. In essence, these realms are both actual places and metaphoric representations of states of being that are not physical but rather outside of both time and space. Since our minds have no easy way to relate to what is beyond the three-dimensional world, the journey experience provides us with a kind of bridge between our ordinary reality and that timeless and formless reality. While journeys may be thought of as metaphoric experiences, they also produce actual and concretely useful information. The Worlds of

Spirit cannot be found using MapQuest, and yet they are also so universally used by shamans—across the spectrum of cultures—that they may be thought of as actual places.[30]

While these realms are part of the spiritual cosmology that functions as a bridge from the ordinary into the extraordinary, that isn't to say that they aren't real. After all, our ordinary, everyday reality is a creation of all the sensory input we have received over our lifetime. It is a kind of collective illusion within which we have learned to operate while in physical form.

We have defined what we see, hear, and touch as reality. However, what we see with our eyes is only a tiny portion of the electromagnetic spectrum that we call visible light. Raptors, like hawks and eagles, and some other animals see below red into the infrared part of the spectrum and so can spot the heat trails left behind by their prey. Many fish, amphibians, reptiles, birds, and even some mammals like rats and mice can see the higher frequency of ultraviolet light. Our hearing only picks up a small range of audible sound, whereas elephants and whales can perceive below that range just as your dog, bats, and other creatures can perceive far above it. Because our perceptions are limited, we require something like a computer interface to help us access the realms beyond our senses. Journey images and places provide the context within which we can receive the information, guidance, and insight we require. The information we receive is often given to us as metaphor to help us grasp that which wouldn't normally be easily understood. That being said, it is also paradoxically true that people all around the world seem to travel to similar places on their journeys. It is as though there is a kind of consensual shamanic reality that gives human consciousness the ability to accept and process the material that is received in the journey state. This consensual shamanic reality and its imagery provide a kind of translation service from the intangible, nonlocal plane that exists beyond time and space constraints and our ordinary way of perceiving.

Figure 4. While diagramming dimensions of reality beyond our own is impossible, this illustration gives a sense of the shamanic cosmos and the interconnections of the realms.

Typically, this consensual shamanic reality or spirit world is divided into levels. These are generally seen as the Upper World, Middle World, and Lower World, although each of these worlds can have many dimensions or levels within them. Nepalese shamans work in the Middle World level most of the time, as it is their point of departure for the other worlds. Your shamanic experiences will also begin in the Middle World.

Preparing to Journey

In traditional shamanism it is understood that the spirit or consciousness of any individual may partially leave the body.[31] Shamans intentionally leave and return for the purpose of discovering hidden information and then imparting the spirit-given wisdom that was gained on the spirit journey to their people.

Therefore, the journey is incomplete without the return to ordinary reality. The tribe does not benefit if the shaman does not come back. In fact, to *remain* in the world of spirit does not benefit *anyone*; the shaman himself is jeopardized. In the shamanic view, when the spirit does not fully return to the body, it causes illness, and if the entire soul is lost, even death. The people who go into the other worlds and do not return, whose psyches remain disassociated, risk illnesses both physical and mental. What separates the madman from the shaman, therefore, is *intentionality*.[32] Your intentionality begins with a clear understanding of all the steps of the journey before you undertake your first experience—and the first step toward a safe practice is realizing that: "It isn't how far you go, it's how fully you return." [33]

While shamanic techniques are relatively simple and the results almost immediate, the evolution an individual undergoes in learning the process is ongoing and profound. Castaneda's Yaqui shaman, Don Juan, refers to the shamanic life as following the "Paths of the Heart." These heart-centered paths draw the most from life and therefore from the travelers as well.[34]

As with ordinary travels, spirit journeys have a starting place. Each of us has found ourselves, at one time or another, in a place in nature that we felt was magical or special. It may have been at the ocean, in a meadow, on a hilltop, or in a quiet wood. In that special place we may have found ourselves feeling particularly safe or filled with joy, or we may have lost all track of time's passing. This is the place where we will initiate our search for entrances into the shaman's reality—to *non-ordinary reality*. It doesn't matter if your spot no longer exists in this reality. As a spirit walker, you will be going *outside* of ordinary realities.

All journeys begin in the Middle World in places that are safe and sacred to the shaman. Finding your sacred places is a perfect introduction to the shamanic realms.

Exercise: A Journey to a Middle World Sacred Place

As you have done with the previous exercises, please read through all the next steps carefully before embarking on your first journey. The preparations you make for this journey will be the same as for your other excursions into the realms of spirit. Before you begin altering your consciousness, please shut off all of your phones and other noisy electronic devices.

For this exercise, you will need:

- A comfortable place to either sit or lie down
- The mp3 audio file of "Shamanic Journey Drumming" and "Call-back Signal" played through headphones
- A blindfold or bandana to cover your eyes
- A notebook and pen to record your experiences

Take the Journey

1. First, situate yourself in your comfortable place and in a comfortable position with your blindfold over your eyes.

2. Put on the headphones and have the recording ready to play but do not start it yet. This recording will help you to expand your awareness into the journey state more easily.

3. Take a few minutes to breathe deeply while quietly assuming the Embodied Light state and then filling yourself with gratitude.

4. Once you have gotten yourself fully into gratitude, allow your memory to take you back to the most magical of your place memories. Choose a place in which you have felt safe. These are often places in nature we have felt to be sacred. Once in that place in your memory, allow yourself to reexperience it with all of your senses.

5. Filled with the strong feelings of your place, begin the "Shamanic Journey Drumming" audio file.

6. While listening to the drumming, engage all of your senses in "being" in your special place. Notice as much as you can. What time of day is it? Where is the Sun or Moon? Is there a breeze or is it still? Are there the scents of flowers, the ocean, pine trees? What is the ground around you like? Be as fully present in this place as you are able. Continue to explore. Get to know the trees, stones, and plants of your power-filled place.

7. At some point in the experience, you will notice that you are accompanied by a friendly animal or bird. Greet this new friend!

8. Spend time in this place until you hear the drumming change to the callback signal.

9. Thank any and all beings who have spent time with you.

10. Return your awareness to ordinary reality by retracing your steps through your place.

11. When the callback is finished, take a deep breath, gently remove your headphones and blindfold, and open your eyes.

Record your experience in a journal with as much detail as you are able. These experiences are sometimes as elusive as dreams and recording them—committing them to concrete memory—will assist you in being able to return to your *sacred place* in the Middle World of Spirit. This place will provide a jumping-off place for journeys to both the Lower and Upper Worlds. As such, it is important to know it well, so take your time with this exercise.

Process Questions

Articulate, as best as you can, in your journal the bodily, emotional, and spiritual sensations of being in your Middle World Sacred Place.

- What did you see? What did you smell?
- Were there any particularly striking features about your special place?

- Think about who you met and what you experienced while there, and write down your impressions.

- Did any part of the experience have a special significance to you?

- Using the Internet or a field guide, spend some time looking up the attributes of the animal or bird that you met in your Middle World Sacred Place.

Chapter 8

The Lower and Upper Worlds

ll of the spirit worlds offer connections that can provide healing, information, and power. However, while spirits that are willing to assist us are found everywhere, the Upper and Lower Worlds are universally populated with trustworthy, compassionate beings of the highest order. It is in these realms that we make the connections with our teachers and protective spirits that can support us.

The Lower World

The Lower World is a realm that is accessed by traveling below or through the Earth and is most often described by shamans as an incredibly vivid, vibrant, and power-filled place. It is a world that resembles the primordial Earth—with unimaginable landscapes and profuse with a diversity of living beings.

The Lower World is also the place where one finds the ancestral spirits of the beings that are found in our world. While the spirits of individual pine trees or black bears reside here in the Middle World, the Universal Spirit of Pine and Spirit of Bear reside in the Lower World. It is as though the Lower World is the spiritual source for nature—only some of which is expressed in physical form at any particular time on the Earth.

As a result, this realm's inhabitants aren't limited to the varieties of animals and plants you might expect. In the Lower World, the spirits of mythical creatures coexist with the spirits of ordinary creatures. Along with every imaginable animal and bird, there are those that have never been physical as well as those that once walked the Earth but are now extinct. On a journey to this realm, it is possible to meet dragons, unicorns, woolly mammoths, centaurs, talking trees, winged horses, dinosaurs, and other fantastic creatures. Our shamanic ancestors most likely shared with their tribe their encounters with these fabulous creatures they found in the Lower World. Spellbound by these shamanic adventures, these people told and retold the stories—thereby breathing these fabled creatures into an existence that falls somewhere between ordinary and non-ordinary reality. All the beings that you meet in the Lower World are safe and available to enter into a spiritual relationship.

To reach the realm of the Lower World, we must enter into and pass through the Earth via animal burrows, openings in hollow trees, caves, deep pools, or man-made locales such as subway tunnels, coal chutes, and mine shafts.

The Upper World

The shamanic Upper World is a realm of spirit above the Middle World that is home to transcendent spirits in human form. The spiritual teachers found in the Upper World make themselves available to answer our questions, guide our steps, and encourage our own inherent inner wisdom. Like Lower World spirits, these teachers exist in the planes of highest existence and so are safe sources of knowledge. These spirits, who have no need for a form, take a shape that is most useful for our interactions, which is most often humanlike in appearance.

Even as you pass through the ordinary Earth to enter the Lower World, you must pass beyond the ordinary sky to enter the

Upper World by such means as riding a hot air balloon, going up in a whirlwind, climbing a beanstalk, climbing a spirit ladder, rising with the sparks from a campfire, or riding a spirit creature.

At some point in the ascent, you will reach a barrier that delineates the end of the Middle World. This boundary may present itself as a rubbery membrane, a distinct ceiling of mist, or a parchment-like surface. Moving through this boundary provides you an entrance to the Upper World.

Since you will be asking questions in the Lower and Upper Worlds, it is necessary to determine if the being with whom you are speaking is your teacher for the question. This is a way to take personal responsibility. You are not meant to blindly follow spirit, but to consciously gather information so that you can choose a clear and informed direction on your own path. You will always have the choice to follow a spirit's advice or not, as your own personal guidance suggests. You never relinquish your free will. Spirit desires active participants who are willing to become conscious partners in the process of living.

Exercise: A Journey to the Lower World

As you have done with the previous exercise in the Middle World, gather your materials and prepare your space for the journey.

Take the Journey

1. First, situate yourself in your comfortable place and in a comfortable position with your blindfold over your eyes.

2. Put on the headphones and have the recording ready to play, but do not start it yet.

3. Take a few minutes to breathe deeply and quietly assume the Embodied Light state and then fill yourself with gratitude.

4. Once you have gotten yourself fully into gratitude, allow your memory to take you back to your special Middle World place.

5. Filled with the strong feelings of your place, begin the "Shamanic Journey Drumming" audio file.

6. Spend time in your place until you feel strongly "there."

7. Repeat this intention to yourself three times: "My intention is to go to the Lower World."

8. Look for a place through which you can enter the Earth for the purpose of going down and through to the Lower World. You may ask the friendly animal or bird you met in the Middle World to help you.

9. Journey downward until you enter the Lower World. This will be a new landscape.

10. Spend time getting to know this realm—making a connection to this new spirit place.

11. Spend time in the Lower World until you hear the drumming change to the callback signal.

12. At the callback, thank any being(s) with whom you have spent time.

13. Return your awareness to ordinary reality by retracing your steps back to your Middle World place.

14. When the callback is through, take a deep breath, gently remove your headphones and blindfold, and open your eyes.

Repeat this journey a few times to get comfortable with your process of getting to the Lower World and the landscape of this new realm. Take as many journeys as you need, and don't get discouraged if it takes some time. Remember you are unlearning your beliefs about what is "real," and you are learning something that feels new. Have compassion with yourself and be persistent. Getting comfortable with the process will help you more easily trust the process as you progress through your studies.

Process Questions

- What is your method for accessing the Lower World?

- Was one of your senses more powerful than the others in the shamanic journey state?

- Did negative feelings intrude upon your process? If so, what were they?

Keep records of what you experience during your journeys so that you can refer to them later. As you continue to practice this exercise, also keep records of what you realize about your own process.

Chapter 9

Power Animals

A *power animal is different* from the animal spirits of the Middle World, being a transcendent spirit that is a teacher, guide, protector, and companion for the shaman. These spirits remind us of a primordial time when people and animals were more closely connected. In her essay, "Rock Art and the Material Culture of Siberian and Central Asian Shamanism," Ekaterina Devlet explains: "A common belief throughout Siberia is that in the mythical, timeless period 'before' the remembered time of human beings (a concept somewhat akin to the so-called Dreamtime of Australian aborigines) there were no distinctions in form or essence between people, animals and birds."[35] The ability of shamans to step outside of ordinary time and space and enter into the timeless world of the spirits allows them access to this deep, ancient kinship bond.

Power animals may take on the form of an animal, bird, or mythic creature. As in the time when there were no real differences between humans, animals, and birds, power animals have the capacity to shape-shift into human form. In the same fashion, the time and space traveling shaman is able to take the shape of a power animal. This shape-shifting is a merging transformation we will discuss more fully later on.

A shaman's power animals are an important source of protection. They are steady companions on your life journey and can provide you with their transcendent wisdom and guidance as well as perform healings on you.

Developing a strong relationship with a power animal will strengthen your own personal sense of being connected to All That Is. In addition, through relationship with this spiritual companion and guide, you will be able to safely traverse all the shamanic realms. With the steadiness and guidance these amazing beings provide, you will be able to step between the worlds with confidence. As you progress through your studies, you will learn to merge with them during any situation to augment your own personal power. However, before any of that, you will need to meet and get to know each other.

As you enter into this exercise, please suspend any prejudice you have about power or presence and allow the right power animal to come to you for this time in your studies. Some people have many power animals and some just one or two, but in either case, the right one at this time in your life and studies may not be what you expect. It is important to remember that no power animals are intrinsically better than another. The spirit of a mouse is as powerful as a bear. A sparrow is as important as an eagle. Each has unique, extraordinary gifts that will be necessary to you as you move through the realms.

Exercise: A Journey to Meet Your Power Animal

As you have done with the previous journey exercises, read through all the steps carefully before you begin. Prepare yourself and your space as for the Lower World journey.

Take the Journey

1. Follow your steps to enter your special Middle World place.

2. Spend time in your place until you feel strongly "there" and engaged with your imagination.

3. As you are in your Middle World place, repeat this intention to yourself three times: "I am going to the Lower World to meet the spirit of my power animal." Let your heart announce this intention to the spirits. Let the gratitude that fills you help you to make a connection by feeling it already done. Do not seek a particular shape or species, simply embody how it feels to have such a steadfast and powerful companion!

4. Look for a place through which you can enter the Earth for the purpose of going down and through to the Lower World. You may ask the friendly animal or bird you met in the Middle World to help you.

5. Journey downward until you enter the Lower World.

6. Keep repeating your heart's intention about meeting the spirit of your power animal. Feel it already accomplished, and while doing so, use all of your senses to look for an animal or bird that is revealing itself to you.

7. You will know when you meet a power animal by noticing an animal or bird that stays close. The animal may greet you, speak to you, or make some other strong form of connection. Be persistent until you meet.

8. Once you meet your power animal, get to know each other by interacting until you hear the drumming change to the callback signal.

9. At the callback, thank the being(s) with whom you have spent time.

10. Return your awareness to ordinary reality by retracing your steps back to your Middle World place.

11. When the callback is through, take a deep breath and gently remove your headphones and blindfold. Open your eyes.

If you didn't meet a power animal initially, don't worry as this kind of work can take some time. Be persistent and keep journeying to the Lower World until you do. Indeed, once you meet this being, you'll want to make numerous journeys to it. You are in the process of developing a power-filled relationship, so each of you must get to know the other. Let your power animal show you around the Lower World. Get to know how it communicates with you and how you are able to understand each other. Be compassionate and gentle with yourself as you learn and practice journeying to your power animal until you feel truly connected with this wonderful being!

As you practice journeying to the Lower World, ask these questions of your power animal:

- "How do I honor you?"

- "How can you help me in my life?"

- "How may we work together in harmony?"

It is also very useful to begin making gratitude offerings to the spirits after receiving guidance from journeying. It is a concrete way to honor that which you have been given and strengthens your connections to the world of spiritual power.

Process Questions

- What was the strongest aspect you noticed about your power animal? Claws, eyes, etc.

- Notice the feelings that you have when you are with this being.

- Did negative feelings intrude upon your process? If so, what were they? Write them down and see if you can get in touch with their source inside of you.

Keep records of what you experience during your journeys so that you can refer to them at a later time. As you continue practicing this exercise, note what you realize about your own process.

Chapter 10

Learning to Ask Questions

As a spirit walker, you always need to have a strong intent for your journeys. This also means that you need a well-formed and heartfelt question in your mind. With such a question, it is much easier to receive a clear, intelligible answer from the spirits. Since Spirit may answer your question with words, images, feelings, a journey within the journey, or in some other way, it is critical to have a plain and precise question so that you can interpret the information you receive.

Our shamanic ancestors relied upon the information that they received in journeys for their survival. As such, they needed to develop relationships with spirit helpers such as their power animals and have clear ways to get information while in the shamanic state of consciousness. If they were facing a critical situation, it would be a waste of time and energy to leave a journey with ambiguous or confusing information.

The journey state essentially functions as a bridge to a world that has none of the typical sensory input our mind commonly uses to process information. The journey is often structured to appear or feel more like the ordinary world, or at least to have enough reference points to provide a familiar context. This allows our human mind to feel more at ease. For instance, even if the landscape of your spiritual realm may appear fantastic or bizarre, you are still provided with a sense of spatial direction—up/down, right/left, and front/back. This gives the mind or personality enough to grasp so that it doesn't feel the desire to either flee or shut down. Instead, what is familiar supports the mind to become curious about new information. In this way, the information, guidance, healing, and insight found in the world of Spirit can be brought over into your ordinary reality.

For those of us living today, accessing the spiritual realms may no longer be a matter of life or death. However, you still want to obtain clear information to your inquiries. For this reason, certain lines of questioning are more effective. The kinds of query that produce the clearest information are questions that begin with one of the following: How? What? Why? Where? or Who? In seeking wisdom, it is also important not to enter a journey with a simple yes-or-no question. This doesn't allow for a solution beyond your original thoughts.

In addition to starting with these forms, it is important to ask a simple question with only one part—that is, one question. If you were using a compound question, you might not know which part of the question is being answered. For the same reason it is best to have only one line of inquiry per journey. In addition, avoid sentences that have an "and/or" aspect. This is especially important if your spirits provide answers through symbolic images.

Here are a few examples to help you better understand how to frame your journey questions.

You may want to know if you should take a new job:

"How can I know if this job is right for me?"

"How will it feel to do this job?"

"What are the consequences of accepting this position?"

"What is the right job for me?"

Perhaps you want to know where to find a new apartment:

"Where is the best place for me to live?"

"What is the best way for me to find my new home?"

"How will I know the right apartment for me at this time?"

"What are the steps to accessing the best place for me to live?"

If you are struggling with confusion about something, you might ask:

"Why am I feeling this way?"

"How can I get clear about ____?"

"What is the best path for me to take to ____?"

Or you may need steps, as in a process or a recipe:

"What are the steps to making ____?"

You can see from these examples that these journey questions each offer a shade of meaning that can help to clarify a situation. By first grounding and meditating, then checking in with yourself, you can get clear about what you really want to know at any given time and for any given journey.

You may have noticed that I didn't include a "When?" question on the list. This is because Spirit operates in a world where there are no clocks or calendars. That isn't to say that you couldn't get advice about timing, however. The best example about this came from a participant who attended one of our workshops many years ago. He was a big-city executive who wanted to find out the best time to move to a new job. This was very important to him in positioning himself to succeed as he timed his steps along the corporate ladder. Since he knew he couldn't ask a "When?" question, he asked, "How can I know the right time to look for a new job?" In his journey he saw the young newlywed he had just hired very pregnant! He knew that when she announced she was going to have a baby, it would be time to start looking for a new position. In this way, the spirits answered a "When?" question without any reliance upon a clock or calendar. Instead they provided a unique time landmark that nevertheless provided clear direction.

Speaking of time, do not rush your spirit work as you are developing relationships with the spirits. Remember to attend to the "Four I's" of living your life:

- *Integrity:* keeping your words and your actions in alignment
- *Integrating* the lessons that you are learning
- *Internalizing* the changes that you experience
- *Implementing* the content of your journeys

The more you work with these principles, the more easily you can rely upon your spiritual connections in difficult situations. Your power as a spirit walker will depend upon how well you come back and integrate the material from your journeys. I would further recommend that you go outside and make a small offering while still in a state of gratitude after each journey. This both honors that you have been given a gift from the spirits and concretely expresses your willingness to be in reverent participatory relationship with them.

Now that you have developed the beginnings of a relationship with your power animal, it is time to practice asking questions in a journey.

Exercise: Asking a Question of Your Power Animal

For this exercise, you will need all of your journey materials.

Take the Journey

1. Get clear about your question and write it down in your notebook.

2. Situate yourself in your comfortable place and in a comfortable position with your blindfold and headphones on.

3. Take a few minutes to breathe deeply and quietly and get into your Embodied Light way of being, and then follow up by getting into your state of gratitude.

4. Once you have gotten yourself fully into gratitude, allow your memory to take you back to your special Middle World place and begin the "Shamanic Journey Drumming" audio file.

5. Repeat your question at least three times as you make your way down to the Lower World. Let your heart announce your intention to the spirits.

6. Meet and greet the spirit of your power animal and ask, "Are you my teacher for this journey?"

7. If the power animal isn't the one to answer your question, ask it to take you to a teacher who can answer your question. Remember to ask the new spirit, "Are you my teacher for this journey?" before you ask your question.

8. Once the power animal or teacher lets you know it is the one to answer your question, ask your question.

9. Allow the power animal or teacher to answer. If something it says or does doesn't make sense to you, ask for clarification until you understand.

10. When you hear the drumming change to the callback signal, thank the spirits, retrace your steps, and return to your starting place as you have done before.

11. When the callback is through, take a deep breath, gently remove your headphones and blindfold. Open your eyes.

12. Record your experiences in your notebook.

Process Questions

- What was it like to ask a question of your power animal? Record your perceptions.

- How did you receive your answer? Make a record of how you perceived the information.

- Did your question lead you to want to ask more questions about the subject? Write them down as questions for future journeys!

Keep records of what you experience during your journeys so that you can refer to them at a later time. As you continue to practice asking questions, note what you realize about your own process as well as what you learn from the spirits.

Now that you have an understanding about asking questions, it is a good time to do an Upper World journey to meet a spirit teacher! You will start in the Middle World as you have done before, but this time you will travel upward. You can call on your power animal to assist you in this journey to meet an Upper World teacher to ask a question. As you did when you asked a question in the Lower World, always discern if the being you meet is the correct teacher by first asking "Are you my teacher?" before broaching your journey question.

Exercise: Upper World Journey to Meet a Teacher

Have a clear question and write it in your journal. As before, prepare yourself and your space. You will begin the journey in your Middle World sacred place and travel upward.

Take the Journey

1. Begin your journey in your Middle World power place.

2. Repeat your question at least three times as you make your way up to the Upper World. Let your heart announce your intention to the spirits. You can take your power animal with you.

3. Once you pass through the boundary into the Upper World, look for a human-form teacher.

4. When you meet a spirit teacher, ask him or her, "Are you my teacher for this journey?"

5. If the teacher isn't the one to answer your question, ask to be taken to a teacher who can answer your question. Remember to ask the new spirit, "Are you my teacher for this journey?" before you share your question.

6. Once this teacher acknowledges his or her role in your journey, ask your question.

7. Once you have asked your question, allow the teacher to answer in his or her unique way. Your answer may be the entire content of the journey, particularly if your teacher replies in metaphor. Your teacher may speak directly to you. You may experience a journey within a journey. Whatever it is, just allow the process to unfold before you. If something doesn't seem to make sense, ask for clarification until you understand.

8. When you hear the drumming change to the callback signal, thank the spirits, retrace your steps, pass back through the boundary into Middle World, and return to your starting place as you have done before.

9. When the callback is through, take a deep breath, gently remove your headphones and blindfold. Open your eyes.

Figure 5. Ban Jhankri is just one of many teachers that a spirit walker could meet in the Upper or Middle Worlds. He initiates Himalayan shamans and is said to be a dwarf who is golden and covered in fur that grows upward. His most unusual feature is that his feet are oriented backward. Acrylic painting on a dyangro.

Process Questions

- What was it like to meet a spirit teacher?

- How did you receive your answer? Make a record of how you perceived the information.

- Did your question lead you to want to ask more questions about the subject? Write them down as questions for future journeys!

As you continue to practice asking questions, keep records of what you realize about your own process. Remember to make a gratitude offering to the spirits after receiving guidance. This is a concrete way to honor that which you have been given, and it strengthens your connections to the world of spiritual power. Your role is to attend to the balance. As you have been given, so you must give from your heart.

Chapter 11

Learning to Shape-Shift: Merging with Your Power Animal

As a part of your training, it is important to learn a shamanic way of remaining spiritually protected. Over my years of practice, I have been kept safe in situations as diverse as healing a possessed person, working near a battlefield, or dealing with the psychic energies left from a homicide. In short, my power animal has allowed me to assist the spirits of those who really needed my help, while preserving my own health and well-being.

In this, as with all things shamanic, there is a reciprocal relationship with the power animal that also extends into merging. Since the power animal is a nonphysical spirit being, the action of merging allows the animal an opportunity to experience the physical world—to be able to move, sniff, eat, and otherwise relish the delights of the body—as a part of its cooperation with the shaman. It involves a blending of energies, consciousness, and on some occasions an actual change in physical form. I think of shape-shifting as a kind of joyful surrender of my ego so that the power animal and I each become something *more* for a little while. There is a magical quality to the experience.

Shamans believe that we are one with everything. This deep kinship with other beings allows us to assume each other's shape and garner each other's wisdom. By so doing, we come away with a different perspective. The illusionary barriers that separate us from the natural world fall away so that we are once again relating to the world in the way of our ancestors.

Figure 6. Winking polar bear. Photo.

As with all that a shaman does, merging begins with a strong intent and is followed by putting energy and action behind it, allowing the intent to actually manifest in the ordinary world. Shape-shifting happens on a continuum from a very subtle merging of senses to a complete transformation into the animal or bird ally. A powerful shaman learns to dance along this gradient to accomplish many different duties.

As you continue down the path of a spirit walker, you will develop your relationship with a power animal and will learn all the different ways you are capable of being together. Since shape-shifting is a continuum of experience, you can begin with learning to merge for protection. This is something I do every day. While merged, I am able to keep my heart center fully open, while remaining safe from other people's intrusive energies. The merged state allows me free access to a deep level of compassion even while in difficult situations. From this place of compassion, it is possible to make much wiser, more informed, and beneficial choices. When combined with your gratitude practice, you will find that merging makes it much easier to be peaceful and loving even in hard times or when surrounded by angry or fearful people.

Let's begin your process of shape-shifting with a journey to merge with your power animal. As before, please read through the instructions before you attempt the exercise.

Exercise: Journey to Merge with Your Power Animal

For this exercise, you will need your usual materials, and you will journey as you have done before to meet your power animal.

Take the Journey

1. Once you meet your animal, ask it, "Please show me how I can merge with you in my daily life for protection."

2. As you are taught how to do this, practice in the journey state.

3. Once you feel like you can merge easily, thank your power animal, unmerge again, and return to ordinary reality.

4. Upon your return, practice merging and unmerging until you can feel the differences between being inside of your power animal and not being merged.

5. When you have finished, make a gratitude offering outside to thank the spirit of your power animal for its guidance and protection. Then you can make notes about the feelings and sensations of being merged.

Exercise: Journey Explorations

- Journey to your power animal to ask it, "In what life circumstances is it best for me to merge with you?"

- Journey to your power animal to ask it, "How does merging with you keep me safe?"

Record the content of your journeys and your perceptions about what you received. After each journey leave an offering outside in gratitude for what you were given.

Exercise: Experiencing Your Power Animal

Now that you have learned the basics of being merged with your animal, it is time to experience more of your power animal's spiritual strength. One of my favorite experiences—and one we always include in our training programs—is being out in nature while merged. If you are a city dweller, you may need to head for a recreation area, a state park, or another public wild spot to fully enjoy this experience. However, your own backyard is an excellent place to begin. Later on, you can scout around to find a safe place in nature where you can explore the landscape and where you are less likely to be interrupted by other people. As with all other exercises, use good sense and discretion in choosing a safe place. For the sake of safety, if your location is remote, please let someone else know when and where you are going.

For this exercise, you will need your usual journey materials.

Take the Journey

1. Journey as you have done before with your eyes closed to meet your power animal.

2. Once you meet the animal, ask it, "Please merge with me so that I can experience this land from your perspective."

3. Once you feel merged, stand up and go out onto the land.

4. Let yourself fully experience the way your power animal sees, feels, smells, and interacts with the landscape. Notice the difference in your senses as you are merged.

5. When you feel full from this experience, play the callback signal, thank your power animal, unmerge again, and return to ordinary reality.

6. Upon your return, take time to sit and remember the sensations. Record them in your notebook.

7. Make a gratitude offering to your power animal and to the land to thank it for holding you both.

Journey Explorations

- Journey to your power animal to ask it: "What are some ways I can honor you for merging with me?"

Record what you received and make sure to follow through with one or more of your power animal's suggestions.

Chapter 12

Your Body as a Sacred Bundle

T hrough the inexplicable vagaries of evolution and unimaginable hardships of famine, hunger, war, and pestilence, our
ancestors managed to pass the sacred gift of physical existence to us. Since the DNA we carry in every one of our cells is like
a library of our biosphere, our bodies may be thought of as a kind
of *sacred bundle*. Much in the way a shaman's sacred bundle or
a medicine bag holds a collection of objects through which a shaman feels a connection to power, the DNA in our cells can remind
us of our connection to all beings and our complete integration
into the body of the Earth. We are inseparably connected with our
home. We live in her body and her body lives inside of us.

Recent scientific discoveries have proved that we *Homo sapiens,* or modern humans, even carry the genetic material of Ne-
anderthals and other branches of the family tree in our DNA.[36]
We aren't as different from our "primitive" ancestors as we once
thought. Indeed, our DNA carries many other surprises. For instance, as much as 8 percent of our DNA is genetic material that
came from viruses. Our mitochondria—the cells' power plants
that convert nutrients into energy—were passed to us from bacteria that entered cells in the primordial sea approximately two
billion years ago. We share genes with every single creature on
Earth that has a backbone—and even some that don't, like the
starfish—since we share a common ancestor that lived over half a

billion years ago. We are in relationship with every being on Earth and those that have been here before us.

Who of the tens of thousands of generations of our ancestors gave us the desire to create beauty or the desire to care for other beings? Which one was the first heart to feel love? As spirit walkers, we can simply ask, because inside of us, all the myriad of beings that have contributed genetic material to us—all of our ancestors—are still alive. When you step into the spirit world in your journeys, these predecessors may be consulted for support and guidance.

My own great, great grandmother is my most trusted spiritual teacher. She has supplied me with amazing support and information over the decades we have worked together. Perhaps Grandma's greatest gift has been to help me to dream a new dream for myself. Many years ago, it was she who first told me of the possibility of transcending our current way of being. She let me know it was possible to become a new kind of human being and that this would support the emergence of a New Earth. Decades ago, when she first said these things to me, they felt beyond the realm of possibility. Over the years and with her gentle and insistent guidance, I have come to know differently, and science has begun to catch up with her early teachings!

These are indeed remarkable times. We are learning so much about what it means to be human and the extraordinary powers that we have. We are starting to remember our place in the cosmos and our capacity to cocreate our reality. For these reasons, I believe that what Grandma told me, so many years ago, is truly correct. This is a very powerful period for human evolutionary potential.

In his book *The Biology of Transcendence*, Joseph Chilton Pearce examines our five neural centers—or brains—four of which are located in the head, while the fifth is located in the heart. He suggests that the dynamic interaction of the head brain (intellect) and heart brain (intelligence) allows us to advance from one evolutionary place to the next. Our heart's ability to connect us to the world of spirit means that our biology has actually prepared the way for us to be transcendent beings. We have the ability to live in both the physical and spiritual worlds in a fully conscious way.

As we are beginning to make these shifts, we are feeling the dissolution of much of what we previously understood. It may be likened to the period of time that a caterpillar pupates into the butterfly. Inside the protective chamber of the chrysalis, the caterpillar secretes enzymes which break its body down into a kind of soup which contains nutrients and imaginal disks. These imaginal disks are undifferentiated building blocks—like stem cells—in that they can become any type of cell. The rich nutrients that were once the caterpillar's body support these undifferentiated cells in growing and creating a completely new organism.

For the metamorphosis of a caterpillar into butterfly to occur, there needs to be a period of *no form*. In the same way, we need to let go of the attachments we have to our old, outmoded ways of perceiving and behaving for a new way of being human to emerge. This can certainly feel a bit uncomfortable since, like the caterpillar, we have no previous experience to help us to know who we are becoming. It may even be as inconceivable as the caterpillar's transition from a soft-bodied, leaf-eating, worm-like creature into a hard-bodied, flying, nectar-sipping insect. Just as none of the caterpillar's previous experience could possibly prepare it for such a change, we have to rely upon something other than our thoughts.

This is where our heart intelligence can come into play, along with the ability to expand our awareness to prepare our psyche for previously unimagined possibilities. The act of expanding awareness creates shifts in our perceptions. In the shamanic state of consciousness and in very deep meditation, we have experiences that create new neural pathways. We gain new insights and ways of looking at reality. This, in turn, supports a shift in our understanding of the world and ourselves so that we gain not only a new perspective but also the opportunity to respond to the circumstances of our lives differently. The new information we receive in an altered or expanded state helps us to attain the bigger view. Just as climbing to an observation deck gives us a new perspective on how a city is laid out, this new vantage point allows us to better understand how things and beings are connected.

The new perceptions that develop also help us to respond differently to the stimulation around us. We have opportunities to think and, even more importantly, *feel* differently in situations. This internal shift has the effect of transforming the situation itself. We have the ability to connect with and affect the invisible world in ways that were once thought of as miraculous.

When talking about miracles, the master Jesus told us, "These things shall you do and greater things than these shall you do also." In addition, he taught his followers that *all* human beings are divine. When we begin to see and feel ourselves as creator beings, we aren't behaving in a heretical way, rather we are following the logical truth which was encoded into our biology and passed to us in the "sacred bundle" of our bodies. We were designed to evolve through our limitations and transform.

When these changes in our selves—and so in our world—more fully emerge, we will have taken the sacred bundle passed to us from all of our ancestors to a new pinnacle of evolution. Maybe the current definitions of humanness and our taxonomical designation will no longer be appropriate. Maybe we will begin to refer to ourselves in a new way. Our species will no longer be *Homo sapiens*, but instead, *Homo transcendentia*—the transcendent human. I can't imagine you and me participating in a more exciting process!

Our ancestors can be an invaluable help in our evolution. Journeying to the beings who contributed to your sacred bundle can help you access information that has been lost, skills that have lain dormant, and wisdom that is timelessly important for today's world. It is especially important if you have not had good connections with your immediate family. Looking further upstream in your genetic river, beyond any immediate familial struggles, you can feel a sense of connectedness and belonging that is so necessary in shamanic work. There are thousands of generations of beings who have gone before you, preparing the way, and each of them has contributed something that has made you uniquely who you are. Their wisdom and perspective can enrich your current life experience. Even though they no longer live, they continue to exist in your body through your genetics and in the spirit world so they can participate in this time of remarkable evolution and change.

Exercise: Meet an Ancestor Who Contributed to Your "Sacred Bundle"

As before, please read all the steps before actually making this journey and gather your usual journey materials before proceeding. Get clear about your intention and write it in your notebook. For this journey your intention is to meet a beneficial ancestor who has contributed to your body's sacred bundle of DNA. Ask: "What is important for me to know about what you gave me?"

Take the Journey

1. Begin in your special Middle World place and call your power animal to you.

2. Once you have connected with your power animal, ask it to take you to "Meet a beneficial ancestor who has contributed to my body's sacred bundle of DNA to ask: 'What is important for me to know about what you gave me? '" This being may present him- or herself in the Upper, Middle, or Lower World. Allow your power animal to guide you.

3. When you meet an ancestor, ask him or her, "Are you my teacher for this journey?" If the ancestor isn't the one to answer your question, ask to be taken to an ancestor who can.

4. Once the ancestor lets you know he or she can answer your question, ask, "What is important for me to know about what you gave me?"

5. Allow the ancestor to answer in whatever unique way is appropriate. If something doesn't seem to make sense, ask for clarification until you understand.

6 When you hear the drumming change to the callback signal, thank the spirits, retrace your steps back to your starting place as you have done before, take a deep breath, and open your eyes.

Process Questions

- What was it like to meet one of your ancestors?
- How did you receive your answer?
- Did your question lead you to want to ask more questions about the subject?

As you continue to practice asking questions, remember to keep records of what you realize about your own process. Remember to make a gratitude offering to the spirits after receiving guidance. As you have been given, so you must give from your heart.

Chapter 13

"Curiouser and Curiouser!"

U p until now, the journeys you have taken may have felt a bit like Alice having her curious adventures in Wonderland. However, the truth is that even here in ordinary reality, the world is really a lot weirder than you might have imagined!

Quantum physics proposes what our shaman ancestors have known for many millennia: everything we know, see, feel, and perceive is connected, and all of what we understand as "solid" or "finite" is actually much more fluid, multidimensional, and mutable.

Indeed, All That Is is not a singular universe. The New Physics understands that our cosmos is a kind of *multiverse* of many parallel dimensions. Shamans have always understood that beyond the reach of our ordinary perceptions there are planes of existence that coexist with our everyday world.

Exploring realms beyond the senses expands the mind beyond its current limitations. In *The Holographic Universe*, Michael Talbot argues that we agree on what is "real" or "not real" because we have believed our senses and have created a *consensus reality*, which has been formulated and ratified at the level of the collective human unconscious at which all minds are infinitely interconnected. By having experiences that undermine the restricted ways we perceive the world and replace these impediments with a more expanded and whole sense of reality, we can begin to shift the perceptual framework that limits all human beings. This naturally happens as all human minds intersect on the levels of consciousness and of spirit.

Keith Floyd, a psychologist at Virginia Intermont College, has pointed out that if the concreteness of reality is but a holographic illusion, it would no longer be true to say the brain produces consciousness. Rather, it is consciousness that creates the appearance of the brain—as well as the body and everything else around us we interpret as physical. In other words, it is our spirit, our vibration, working through the medium of consciousness—our thoughts and feelings—that crystallizes vibration into physical matter.

Figure 7. The Multiverse. Digital painting.

The book *Gifts of Unknown Things*[37] outlines the remarkable experiences the biologist Lyall Watson had on an island in Indonesia. First published in 1976, it describes Watson's encounter with a shaman woman who, by performing a ritual dance, was able to make an entire grove of trees instantly vanish into thin air. While he and another astonished onlooker continued to watch, she caused the trees to reappear, then disappear again several more times.

We are beginning to get a clearer understanding of how this can work. A growing number of scientists from diverse disciplines believe that the most profound implication of the holographic paradigm of the universe is that there are *no limits to the extent to which we can alter the fabric of reality*. So, not only is the Indonesian shaman's feat plausible, it implies that even more amazing accomplishments are possible. In order to experience a different kind of reality, we need to change our consciousness. Doing this will allow us to reprogram what we have created as the material world.

The first order of business is to change your fundamental perceptions of reality by opening the mind to the possibility that other realities exist. Begin to ask your trusted power animal or teacher to give you mind/heart-expanding experiences in your journeys. Extreme and altered states can provide a kind of spaciousness to our consciousness that allows us to "dream bigger." Indeed, when teaching my students, I do not talk about altering ordinary consciousness, rather I suggest that *the shamanic state of consciousness is an expanded state of awareness or perception which produces an altered experience of reality*. When we know something else is possible, we can begin to make it real.

When you have a conscious, unshakable understanding of how reality works—through having had experiences in the shamanic state of consciousness—and have a way of mastering the "inner technology" of your feelings, you can begin to generate a life of greater harmony, peace, and healing. As you understand that the world that you once believed was "real" is not as solid as the world of your thoughts and feelings, then your entire sense of reality begins to shift.

A study reported in *Science Daily* in 1998 described how a research team at the Condensed Matter Physics Department of the Weizmann Institute of Science conducted a highly controlled experiment demonstrating how a beam of electrons is affected by the act of being observed. The experiment revealed that the greater the amount of "watching," the greater the observer's influence on what actually takes place.[38] This makes good sense if we are actually *creating* particles and their behaviors with our consciousness.[39]

Being a spirit walker means living with a great deal more discipline, as your limited human senses will continue to spin an illusionary vision of reality in your mind even as you are in the process of weaving a different one. If old beliefs or perceptions challenge your desired new experience, work through them with the help of your spirit teachers and with human support when necessary. Let the knowledge that you are cocreating your experiences fuel your desire to keep going forward with whatever is necessary to completely "change your mind" and so transform your world.

Time Has Depth

Our *consensus reality* experience of time needs to be altered as well. Time is not the singular, linear concept we have accepted. Instead, it is inseparable from space and is also expressed as a multiplicity. Just as there are multiple parallel dimensions, each of these dimensions has multiple possible pasts, presents, and futures—that is, many different possible time streams. You can think about this as time's depth. In addition, these streams of time occur simultaneously. Grandma once described time like stations on the radio. She said all of them are playing all of the time, and yet we only are ever tuned in to one. As we can spin the dial to find different stations, so too can we tune in to different experiences in time.

Journeying is a method by which you can go with a trusted teacher to other streams of the present to open up your mind to new possible futures for yourself.

Exercise: Suggested Journeys

Ask your teacher or power animal to help you have expanded experiences of reality. Follow these lines of inquiry in separate journeys and work with your own teachers and power animals to get a visceral understanding of this material. Since it is our feelings that have the greatest power to make positive changes in physical reality, it is essential to "feel" the information. Do these kinds of expansive journeys often and ask your teachers how you can continue to expand your awareness to augment the information spun by your senses—while remaining grounded in this reality. Remember, it is being fully present in this reality while feeling your new perceptions that will actually change this reality!

- Have your teacher or power animal give you a *felt* experience of the "sea of radiance" that is the true fabric of reality.
- Ask to have a safe, *felt* experience of parallel universes—the multiverse.
- Ask to have a safe, *felt* experience of time's multiplicity.

As you practice expanding your perceptions, remember to ground afterward and do an offering in nature. Keep records of what you experience in the journeys and what you realize about your own process. Give thanks for your physicality and your capacity to feel, as these are essential to a shaman's power.

Process Questions

- How has your new shamanic understanding of All That Is benefited aspects of your daily life?

- How does your new understanding differ from the way you felt about the world before you began to journey into the world of the spirits?

- What aspects of your thinking or perception do you believe still need to evolve and change?

Develop journey questions to begin getting the support you need to shift.

Chapter 14

Breath, Song, and Prayer

To be alive, **you must breathe**, and to be a spirit walker, you must also learn to pray and sing. A shaman understands the interconnected dance between spirit and breathing and uses breath in a sacred manner. Human beings may equate the "drawing of the last breath" with the exit of one's spirit from form, and it is true that without breath, we die. However, it could just as easily be argued that it is spirit which functions as the basis of the breath of life since it is the essential "something" that animates the physical form. Whichever way you choose to look at this conundrum, it is clear that breathing is intimately connected with our physical and spiritual existence.

Breathing as a Shamanic Activity

Just as physical matter arises from the potential *expressed through vibration,* one of the ways we are able to manifest spirit is through the vibrations of our marvelous human voice. Our voice expresses our thoughts and our feelings, making them tangible, and so we are able to continually recreate our physical world.

Every aspect of being alive begins with our breath. Our first cry as a newborn is a declaration of our presence in the world. However, the act of sharing our thoughts and feelings is what gives that presence form, shape, and expresses its purpose. To do this, we transform breath into audible sounds.

Tribal shamans recognize that in order to be a person of power, it is necessary to work with breath as a part of healing, chanting, and as an aspect of daily restoration. For this reason, a spirit walker cultivates the ability to breathe deeply and with intention as a preparation for using the voice as a shamanic tool.

Exercise: Breath Journey

While there are many different spiritual practices that involve very specific breathing exercises, it is important to discover and put into action what breathing practice is uniquely useful to you. The next exercise is a journey process to access wisdom about the breath directly through your helping spirits.

As you have done with the previous exercises, follow all the preparation and procedural steps for the journeys. Do each one of these journeys individually and take time to integrate the information you receive before going on to the next. At the end of each journey, remember to ground yourself, make an offering, and carefully record your experiences in your notebook.

Breath Journey Questions

- Journey to a teacher or power animal to ask, "Show me how my breath connects me to All That Is."

- Journey to a teacher or power animal to ask, "Please give me a breathing exercise that can safely invigorate my body."

- Do a follow-up journey to a teacher or power animal to ask, "When are the best moments for me to use the invigorating breathing exercise?"

Include this exercise into the other shamanic practices you have already learned. Remember to do them all until they become second nature to you. This process of integrating the exercises is changing you in ways that will take time for you to notice. Be patient with yourself and also persistent in your practice.

Shaman Songs

Our voices and our ability to speak are a fundamental part of our intrinsic humanness. As an outgrowth of our ability to speak, song has been used throughout our human evolution to effect comfort and healing. Children around the world are sung to sleep and soothed by their mothers' voices. This is a cross-cultural phenomenon with roots extending deeply into our early human development.

Most shamans utilize singing, storytelling, or some other sort of vocalization in their work. Some use song as a way to shift their consciousness. Many also use a rattle, drum, or other instrument to accompany their songs. The Sami shamans of the Scandinavian high arctic provide a unique example of the shamanic vocalizations in their highly stylized singing called a *joik*, to honor the spirits of the natural world. Each *joik* is an individual "song" which "sings" a particular spirit. These songs are not seen as describing the spirit but rather as a sung manifestation of the spirit itself. The sounds in a *joik* may be actual words, but many times are repeated syllables such as *la, lo, lu, jo, ho,* etc.

As part of his healing work, the Sami shaman or *noaidi* would use ritual *joiking* as well as drumming to enter into the realm of the spirit. The *joik* would bring the spirits to the ceremony and in effect open a doorway into their invisible world. The *noaidi* would *joik* each spirit he encountered, use *joiking* to drive away unwanted spirits, and also voice the patient's spirit song to coax back an errant soul for healing.

Joiking as a form of spirit interaction was seen as so powerful that during the eighteenth and nineteenth centuries, the Christian church banned it entirely. Like drumming, it was seen as a heathen activity. As with many other tribal people who were persecuted in such a manner, the Sami pushed their shamanic ways underground to keep them safe. It was only during the latter half of the twentieth century that *joiking* was seen as acceptable by society again, and it is practiced today by contemporary Sami people. Whether sung by a reindeer herder or a performer, the Sami *joik* about all parts of their existence. They give voice to the spirits of their favorite reindeer, a special birch tree, their home, the bear, their family group, and others in their spiritual landscape. It is an activity that was once intertwined in all parts of traditional Sami life and is returning to full acceptance once again.

Other people of Europe have also used versions of this technique. The Icelandic sagas chronicle how the ancient Norse/Germanic shamanic seeresses, or *völvas,* used singing as well as drumming to support their shamanic journey state. The singing was done not only by the seeress, but by a chorus of other women who knew the sacred songs. These song-supported journeys could last for many hours.

Shamanic chanting is, in some cultures, the primary way of making a connection with the helping spirits. In a shamanic journey, the shaman receives a song to sing to call upon the helping spirits. Finnish ethnologist Kai Donner describes such a theory of the shaman's spirit songs when detailing a ritual among the Selkup people of Western Siberia:

> The drum echoes more and more intensely, and the shaman . . . gradually begins to murmur something in a distant and strange voice. Soon he begins to hum a tune. . . . He summons his [spirits] and when, the noise of the music steadily increasing, they finally arrive, he requests their help.

The shaman continues to use song to express the information he receives from the spirits, who "begin to speak, explaining to him what he desires to know. He sings what they say, or to be more precise they speak through him." [40]

Indeed, my Ulchi teacher, Grandfather Misha, sang all of his shamanic journeys. He would use song as a part of empowering himself, calling the spirits, and in healing others. As he sang, it was possible for those who were with him to experience the places and beings he visited while he was in the spirit world.

Tuvan shamans practice a vocal art known as "throat or overtone singing." This strange and haunting form of vocalization, which is very widely practiced in the Central Asian republic of Tuva, sounds very similar to the overtone chanting of Tibetan monks. With practice, the throat singer can produce three notes simultaneously.

When practiced by a shaman, these otherworldly sounds can be used for spiritual purposes. Ai Churek used sound extensively in her shamanic healing practice. As with the Sami, a Tuvan shaman sings the songs of the spirits, using her voice to bring them forth and direct them to their work. During a healing ritual, which may last up to three hours, she alternated her singing between a more ordinary sounding song and the vibratory overtone style of throat singing. When her normal singing voice shifted into throat singing, her voice deepened to a growling bass with several higher, crystalline-sounding overtones blended throughout. A Tuvan shaman may also combine throat singing with vocal imitations of animals during a healing.

Learning to use your voice in a mindful fashion is a part of becoming a spirit walker. It is yet another way that you can become a force for positive change in your own life and for All That Is. Shamans realize that using their voice can magnify the power of intention. Using your voice can strengthen your interaction with the spirits, make clear your intent, and support a deepening of your relationships.

Figure 8. Tuvan shaman, Ai Churek singing and drumming during a ritual in 2004. Photo: © 2004 & 2012 Carl A. Hyatt.

Shaman Power Song as Prayer

Shamans around the world have special songs to empower themselves and reinforce their connection to the helpful and healing spirits on whom they depend. These may be referred to as a shaman's "spirit" or "power" song. These songs usually have a distinct melody and may either have clearly understood words as in a true song or a series of sung syllables or tones.

Power songs provide you with a way to immediately connect yourself to helpful spirits. Practicing your power song aloud is the best way to fully embody it so that you can recall it in any circumstance. Humming the melody of my song was beneficial during an emergency trip to the hospital for a member of my family. In spite of the harrying energies that swirled around me, the simple humming of the tune brought me back to balance quickly, and in turn, my centeredness calmed those around me. It also became easy to access the spiritual help I needed to support my loved one.

As you diligently practice your connection, gratitude, the rituals I've given you, and your power song, you will find that you are actually transforming the fabric of your being. While subtle at first, over time you will find that you hold your center more easily, are less distracted by your fears or frivolous, mindless activities, and have a much deeper experience of joy in your life. It may seem paradoxical, but working with spirits in this way also helps you to be much more connected and "plugged in" to the Earth plane. This shift in your way of being puts you in harmony with the energy of the natural world. It also allows you to have more wildlife sightings in nature as the animals and birds will no longer perceive you as potentially harmful or destructive. This recognition by the creatures in nature contributes to the helpful spirits in the Middle World being more willing to engage, as well.

Exercise: Power Song

For the next exercise you will be doing two journeys. Prepare yourself as you have done before and have your notebook handy to record what you receive. Since you are going to be asking the spirits about a song, it would be especially useful if you had a way to capture the sounds/song so you will be able to remember it. A small digital recorder works well for this purpose.

Journey Questions to Receive a Power Song

- Journey to a teacher or power animal to ask, "What is my power song?"
- Journey to a teacher or power animal to ask, "Under what circumstances do I use this power song?"

Immediately after returning from the first journey, sing this song for half an hour to fully internalize it. Once you are finished singing, you can write your notes and observations. After making notes, give an offering to the spirits. Since the voice and the element of Air are so intimately related, please speak out loud as you make your offering. You may also wish to toss cornmeal into the breeze, burn incense, shake a rattle, or ring a small bell to accompany your voice.

Once you have learned and practiced your power song, journey to the same teacher and ask the second question.

Process Questions

- What was it like to receive a power song from your teacher or power animal?
- What was it like to sing your song aloud?

Chapter 15

The Middle World

L earning to work well and safely in the Middle World is a necessary part of being a powerful shamanic practitioner. To accomplish this, the spirit walker must develop a clear and certain relationship with the beings of nature—the spirits of plants, birds, and animals—as well as those transcendent spirits that are unique to the Middle World. This is critical because this is also the place of *manifestation*, that is, where the formless spiritual energies develop physicality or become embodied.

Not only living beings, but also the energies of thoughts and desires are physically manifested. It is the place where the "Word" is made "Flesh," where quantum vibration becomes physical matter. For this reason, we need to be able to work both safely and with humility in this realm. The Middle World is where, in our unconsciousness, human beings have manifested the unbeneficial energies that need to be rebalanced.

The Middle World is also where the disembodied spirits of the dead, negative emotional energy, and other spiritual and physical hazards reside. While the Middle World is where we need to focus our attentions to create harmony and balance in our lives, we need to learn to do this safely and with discernment. For these reasons, it was necessary for you to make strong connections with protective, helpful, and healing spirits in the Lower and Upper Worlds before doing more work in the Middle World. Now that those are in place, you can begin exploring.

As I stated earlier in the book, the Middle World is where the many wise and ancient spirits of nature live. These are the spirits of all the plants, animals, and birds as well as the spiritual beings that our ancestors honored and with whom they worked in partnership. They are the green men and women, the fairies, plant devas, gnomes, elves, and other elemental nature spirits who are particularly tuned in to the Earth and her many shifts and changes. A shaman may access the spirits of the Middle World to share their power. They can assist us in bringing ourselves and our environment back into harmony.

Figure 9. Earth from space. Photo: NASA.

Our planet is in a constant state of rebalancing and harmonization. The surface crust, ever restless in its movements, constantly involutes and erupts, changing the face of the land. When the Earth's surface rises and falls or the waters surge over the land, we humans, in our illusionary preeminence, experience these shifts and changes as catastrophes. We interpret these natural movements as raging planets or savage seas, holding the idea, from our limited perspective, that the Earth is somehow cruel. Unlike other species, we try to make the Earth into a tame and docile thing, forgetting her immense power as well as our own limitations. The Middle World realm is where the elemental forces of Air, Water, Fire, and Earth dance as a part of the planet's continual recreation of her physical body. Every aspect of our physical nature is a gift from the elementals and even our bodies themselves are fashioned from their dance.

The elements are in a constant dance of interrelationship working together to keep the engine of creation going and to keep us alive! Air circulates as wind in the atmosphere and, by gathering up Water, brings us rain. Water, which is heated by Fire—the Sun—helps to fuel those same air currents that carry us the weather. Fire has the capacity to stir up great, rushing winds, yet it cannot exist in the absence of Air. Through her many landscape features, the Earth can coax the rain from a cloud with a mountain face or encourage the wind through a canyon. Earth's soil, which itself is a mixture of both eroded rock and organic material from deceased plants, works with Water to nourish the growth of trees and plants which enrich Air with necessary oxygen. Through these few examples, you can begin to see the complexity of the world to which we belong.

As someone who desires to be a person of power, you know you need to be more connected to nature, but often you may not be exactly sure how to go about it. After all, nature is an enormous playing field. If you think about how much richness and complexity we have to work with in nature, it can become completely overwhelming. To help make developing a relationship with each of the spirits easier, it is important to learn about them individually while simultaneously holding on to your understanding of their relationships with each other.

A Sanctuary in Your Own Backyard

Supporting a healthier ecosystem in your own yard can be a huge step toward improving our collective environment. Your focused actions are a part of your spiritual practice and a means to produce harmony.

The National Wildlife Federation has a wonderful incentive for individuals and families who are searching for ways to improve their local ecosystem in the Backyard Wildlife Habitat program.[41]

Creating a healthy, wildlife-friendly yard includes several features. Besides eliminating synthetic pesticides and herbicides, feeding the birds and offering them a clean water source will attract many more species. Even if you are an apartment dweller, you can work in your community to support healthy places for wildlife using these guidelines.

- It is important to wildlife that we grow native vegetation on our land, especially since so many yards are filled with non-native imported species that aren't good food sources for our birds and animals. Local, native shrubs, trees, and plants that produce acorns, berries, and other seeds supply food for wildlife. You can also supplement natural food sources by locating bird feeders in your garden.

- Wildlife needs a constant, reliable source of water to thrive. You can provide this with a birdbath, pond, or even a shallow dish. Wildlife will use water for both drinking and bathing so a side benefit of providing water will be the treat of watching birds splash around in your birdbath!

- Good cover protects wildlife against the elements and predators. Create cover for wildlife with densely branched shrubs, hollow logs, rock piles, brush piles, stone walls, evergreens, and meadow grasses.

- It's important to offer your local wildlife safe places for courtship and nurturing young. Mature trees can provide den sites for squirrels and nesting places for birds. Having trees or shrubs that host caterpillars will ensure the presence of butterflies in your habitat. Salamanders, frogs, and toads will thrive in a pond or water garden.

- The way you garden or manage your landscape impacts wildlife in your yard and your entire neighborhood. Planting native flora, eliminating chemicals, reducing areas dedicated to lawn, and building healthy soil are just some of the things you can do to help wildlife and conserve natural resources. Even simple changes can make a difference.

Figure 10. Backyard habitat sign.

When we begin treating our yards as sacred land and honoring the creatures and spirits that reside there, we begin tipping the balance back to health for ourselves and for the planet. Not only that, our yards can become a doorway to the powers in the Middle World as well as a source of delight and joy when we witness the diversity of life around us growing and flourishing.

Once my partner and I certified our small, in-town yard, we began to keep track of the different species that either visited or made their homes around our house. Paying attention to our "neighbors" has given us a deeper sense of joy in realizing how many other living beings share our little part of the world. We have cataloged more than sixty different bird species alone! Once you add the twelve or so wild mammals, several amphibians, reptiles, innumerable insects, and all the native plant species using our land—you quickly realize how much home and garden care can become a personalized form of Earth stewardship. While we might feel it's hard to create change on a global scale, we can certainly make sure that our local garter snake has a safe place to warm itself in the sun, that the pine siskin will find food on its midwinter fly-through, and that the toads will have ample shade during a hot stretch in July.

This all has a greater significance for spirit walkers since we understand that all that is living is part of our family. A profound part of spirit walking is reacquainting yourself and developing relationships with the larger family to which you belong. This requires that you first introduce yourself to the inhabitants of the Middle World. This realm is populated not only by those beings that you already know as alive but also by an enormous diversity of other kinds of beings. As you enter into relationship and attend to connections with them, you will begin to understand how your thoughts, feelings, and choices impact their health and well-being. You will also gain a deeply felt, intuitive sense of how you are affected by those interconnections.

The rich tapestry of Earth is the result of both the reshuffling of genetic material and the dreaming of many interconnected beings. Immersing yourself in the field of dreaming—the world of consciousness and spirit—is a way to deeply connect to the heart of all life, an adventure that unfolds here in the Middle World.

The Square Yard

A thorough study our planet's diverse and complex ecosystems is a very involved and lifelong quest. To begin establishing a sacred relationship with the natural world, we need a simpler way to approach it that excites our curiosity without leaving us overwhelmed. One method that I've found useful is creating a dedicated square yard of space on your land. This plot of earth can function like a sacred portal for you into the greater whole while remaining manageable in scale—a tiny sanctuary in a busy world.

To begin working with your square yard, you will need to gather a few items to support your observations:

- A magnetic compass
- Four sticks, approximately 12 inches long
  Foot-long lengths of half-inch dowel from the hardware store work well for this purpose. With a knife, carefully sharpen one end of each stick or dowel into a point. If you are anything like me, you may wish to paint these sticks or decorate them in some fashion. Just make sure that you use nontoxic paint and decorations which are both wildlife friendly and will withstand being outdoors for a year.
- Ball of twine
- A sketchbook (9 by 12 inches or larger)
- Graphite drawing pencils
- Colored pencils (a set with 48 to 96 colors)
- A sharpener for your pencils and something to catch the shavings

- A white plastic artist's eraser
- A magnifying glass
- A ground cloth to sit on
- Field guide(s) of your local region
  I recommend that you start with a good all-purpose, more generalized field guide such as the *National Audubon Regional Field Guide*[42] for your area. This type of guide offers the widest selection of flora and fauna in a single volume. As you continue your study, you can add more guides that specialize in a particular family of organisms such as mammals, mushrooms, trees, and the like.
- A day pack or bag to hold all of your supplies
- A few other things
  While the following items are not essential to beginning your study, they are handy additions to your observation kit: large *paper clips* to hold down the pages of your sketchbook which can tend to lift in the breeze, a *ruler* for making straight lines and measuring the size of the objects in your square yard, *binoculars* to identify the birds flying around you, and finally, a *hat with a brim* to keep the sun off your head and out of your eyes when drawing outdoors.

Finding Your Square Yard

Begin by choosing a place on your land or in your yard that won't be disturbed by activities such as pedestrian traffic or lawn mowing. Look for a place that borders several different kinds of areas—such as one that encompasses a garden *and* lawn or in a meadow area *and* around a tree. Place your sharpened sticks or dowels in the ground so that they form the corners of an area that is roughly a yard square. You may want to place your sticks in the cardinal directions. Once you are happy with the sticks' locations, run a length of your string around the sticks to form an area that is marked off from the rest of the land. The resulting plot is your observation area and may be considered your own sacred space. This area is meant to remain set up for at least a full year so you will have ample time to get to really know the wonder and beauty held just inside the string.

Exercise: Begin Working with Your Square Yard

Begin by sitting down next to your square yard. While in the Embodied Light state, make a small offering prayer to thank the spirits of this place for their willingness to share themselves with you. Let yourself tune in to the place and engage all of your senses as you do in a journey. Make notes in your notebook about what you experience. Take time to record all that you felt, saw, and heard. Articulate, as best as you can, in your sketchbook/journal the bodily, emotional, and spiritual sensations you experience.

Begin observing what is in your square yard. Take time to sketch what you see. Don't worry about how well you draw. Simply record what you see as best as you can. This sketchbook/journal of your square yard is just for you! Enjoy playing with the colored pencils and have a good time with your observations. Notice all the plant life, insects, and animal signs that are in your space.

Repeat your observations on a regular schedule. Make time to observe your sacred space at least once a week. Record all the changes that you notice and all the species that you encounter.

When you really take the time to observe it, you'll be surprised how much happens in even a small plot of the natural world. Even a typical suburban yard can hold a wide variety of life if you refrain from using synthetic fertilizers, pesticides, fungicides, and herbicides.[43] Once you have seen and identified the inhabitants of your square yard, you may want to have your power animal help you to meet some of them. Be patient and work with one species at a time.

Journey Explorations

- Ask your power animal take you to meet one of the plants in your square yard. When you meet the plant, ask its name—what it prefers to be called—and ask it if it has any message for you.

- Also ask your power animal how you can begin a mutually beneficial relationship with that being.

- Repeat this journey with any animals, insects, birds, and trees in your square yard. Upon your return from each journey, remember to make an offering of gratitude.

- Check in with your square yard at least once a week for a year. Go through all the seasons and develop a sense of who and what makes their home or visits your little patch of Earth!

Process Questions

- What did you learn about the land near your home by working with your square yard?

- How does this differ from the way that you understood the land before you worked with your square yard?

- What has it been like to create a backyard wildlife sanctuary?

- What "new" family members have you met in this process?

Chapter 16

The Wider Landscape of the Middle World

You have already begun a deeper exploration of the Middle World through your square yard exercises. Now it is time to broaden your vision to get a sense of your *spiritual* position on the Earth!

In approaching the Middle World, I find it is best to begin with learning how to honor the Spirits of the Directions. Like the explorers of centuries past, we must have a sense of direction prior to embarking into new territories. We need to understand where we stand spiritually on the Earth—a deeper sense of location than what GPS coordinates provide—and this sense unfolds with understanding more about the spiritual dimensions of place and how to create sacred space.

The Circle of Life Is Actually a Sphere

For indigenous peoples, the spirits of the directions are acknowledged in all facets of life and honored in religious ceremonies. The directions of the East, South, West, and North have their own powers and are houses for spiritual energy. Many native traditions also honor the directions of up, down, and the center. Taken together, these seven directions provide a spiritual sphere in which all life on Earth is held. While we know scientifically that the Earth herself is a sphere, we largely experience her body as a surface plane on which we live our lives. By thinking of the directions in terms of a sphere, we are in effect also declaring that the Earth is held in space as much as we are. It is a perspective that can not only help provide a context for our lives, but also provide a way to see that the Earth sits within the larger contexts of the solar system, Milky Way galaxy, and Universe. The entire cosmos becomes an endless series of interconnected spheres within spheres.

Each culture perceives the Spirits of the Directions in different ways. For instance, East may be thought of as a place of new beginnings, the place of rain, the birthplace of the morning sun, or the direction of unity, success, or triumph—depending upon the specific traditions of different indigenous groups. While you may appreciate and honor the traditions of another culture and even perform those rituals for which you have been properly instructed, it is important not to take them as your own. Each tribal society has its own intellectual and cultural capital that is an integral part of its survival. It is improper to appropriate another culture's rituals and traditions. What is important is for you to develop your own connections to the directions.

Exercise: The Wisdom of the Directions

Prepare for each of these journeys as you have done before, and go on separate journeys for each direction as indicated below. Upon your return at the callback signal, take ample time to remember and record your journey experience in your notebook. After each journey, go outside and make an offering of thanks. In these journeys, you may wish to face the direction about which you journeyed. Let your heart fill with gratitude for the gifts you have received and place your offering on the Earth with reverence.

Journey Questions

- "What is the wisdom of the direction of the East?"
- "What are the stories you can share with me about this direction?"

- "How did my ancestors understand this direction?"
- Repeat this journey for the South, the West, the North, the Center, the Upward/Sky, and the Below/Earth directions. Do each one separately.

You may wish to also ask your teachers about the other points of the horizon such as the Northeast, the Northwest, the Southeast, and the Southwest. After each journey, make notes about the feelings you had about each direction. At this point, it would also be great to think about your personal experiences with the directions. Perhaps you were born north of where you now live, or you remember a particularly potent experience with a sunset in the western sky. Review all of your most precious directional memories around the Circle, at the Center, Up, and Down. Record all of them in your notebook as well.

Exercise: Honoring the Directions

Since the directions define the sphere of existence, it is important to honor their role in your life. Our star, the Sun, rises and sets in a prescribed place along the horizon wheel as does the Moon and the other celestial bodies. The winds blow over the surface of the world from their own place on that same wheel. The birds and animals migrate from one direction to another. All life on Earth is held within the embrace of the directions.

As every indigenous tradition has its own understanding of the powers and stories of the directions, each of them also has specific rituals for honoring their circle. Typically, the act of honoring the directions is an essential component of ceremonies and of creating sacred space. These kinds of rituals are a way of declaring a specific moment and time within the larger space of existence.

As you have done before, perform the journeys indicated below. When you are through, go outside and perform your ritual of honoring the directions. If you were told that you need a specific tool, such as a rattle or cornmeal, don't worry if you don't have it just yet. Use what is at hand right now. An aspirin bottle makes a great impromptu rattle, or a piece of your lunch can stand in for cornmeal. What is important is to practice the ritual right away to help you really internalize its details. The accoutrements can arrive in your life later.[44] Once you have completed your ritual, let your heart fill with gratitude for the gifts you have received and make an offering of thanks.

Take the Journeys

- "What is my personal ritual for honoring the Spirits of the Directions?"
- "In what situations do I honor the directions with my ritual?"

Exercise: Creating Sacred Space

As you continue your study of spirit walking, there will be times when you will be asked to create an intentional sacred space. This is the action of erecting a spiritually potent container for specific shamanic work, and knowing how to do this is an important aspect of your shamanic skill set. Creating an intentional sacred space provides safety for a ritual, declares the importance of a ceremonial action, and can even provide a ritual framework for your daily prayers.

While quite often the honoring of the directions is a part of such a ritual, it is important not to assume that your spirit teachers want you to do it in that fashion. Instead, take the time to journey about finding your own personal ritual for creating intentional sacred space.

Take the Journeys

- "How would you like me to create intentional sacred space?"
- "Under what circumstances do I use this ritual?"

Process Questions

- What does it feel like to be able to dedicate a sacred space?
- How does the ritual change your perceptions of the location?
- Think about how this practice could benefit your daily life. Record your impressions.

Articulate, as best as you can, in your journal the bodily, emotional, and spiritual sensations of what you experienced in your journeys.

Chapter 17

Ceremony and Prayer

reating and leading an effective and powerful ceremony are one of the traditional functions of a shaman. Whether for oneself or for a group, ceremony has the effect of making the intangible more real. The word "ceremony" comes to the English language from the Latin, *caerimonia,* which refers to a "sacred rite or ritual."[45] While this word may conjure up high religious rites or rigidly prescribed forms of conduct, a ceremony is different for the shaman. For spirit walkers, ceremony becomes a way of life, a way of behaving in the world that can, on occasion, be formalized. In these cases, a specific need has arisen that requires the coalescing and direction of energy toward a purpose. Whether formal or more casual, the elements involved in enacting a powerful ceremony are largely the same. They include having a clear, heart-centered intent, preparing the space, setting the stage, calling together the participants—both seen and unseen—opening the energies, directing the flow, and closing.

Essential Elements of a Safe and Powerful Ceremony

Having clear intentions. This is the beginning place for all rituals or ceremonies and also for each day. What is your focus? Starting the day with a grateful heart is a great beginning, but in what way do you choose to utilize your energy? This step is often missing in everyday life. Selecting a focus, setting your intention for your day, can transform the way it unfolds. I am not suggesting a micromanagement approach that includes a rigid schedule, but rather choosing the direction through an intent. As I stated earlier, feelings are what manifest in the physical world. As you are able to transmute your disruptive feelings, fill with gratitude, and project feelings that you wish to manifest, you will begin to experience your life in a very different way. In continually working with your feelings, you effectively put an overlay of ceremony on even the most mundane of tasks and, in essence, make every action sacred.

For a ceremony that includes others, it is especially necessary to have a razor-clear intent. This allows all the participants to more fully contribute their energy and excitement to the desired outcome. For instance, in a wedding ceremony the clear intent allows the gathered community to emotionally and physically participate in the joining of the couple. Even when the specific parameters of the ritual are unfamiliar, a clearly defined intent makes it easy for those gathered to weave themselves into a group.

Clearing and preparing the space. We have a dear friend who follows the Red Road and has been a sundancer and Lakota ceremonialist for many, many years. Preceding every one of her community's ritual gatherings, the space that will contain the ceremony is subjected to a thorough cleaning. She makes sure that the windows are washed, the floor is swept and mopped, and every surface in the space gleams. As she and her helpers go about this work, she sings sacred songs—because her cleaning work isn't *preparation for* the ceremony but rather a *part of* the ceremony itself. This aspect is a way to clear the slate so that what follows is uncluttered with either physical obstructions or disruptive energy.

If you desire to step into the life where all is sacred, how do you clear away what has gone before that is unbeneficial to this day's flow? It is possible to use your morning time of showering and brushing your teeth as way to enact a sacred cleansing of yourself. Rather than mindlessly stepping into the shower, washing your hair, or lathering up for a shave each day, you can dedicate these times to a sacred clearing away and personal blessing.

I use my shower time as a way to reconsecrate myself and rededicate my heart to my path. In fact, every time I wash my hands or shower I allow myself to feel it as a sacramental act. It is an opportunity to remind myself through gratitude of my own sacredness, both as a physical being and as a timeless, eternal part of All That Is. Once in the flow of gratitude, I also honor the elements that make the shower possible. I thank the water for carrying away that which I do not need and providing me with most of my physical form. I thank the warm air for surrounding me and giving me breath and the fire for providing the hot water. I end with gratitude for all life as I turn off the taps.[46]

When setting the stage for a more formal ritual, the idea is the same. The space needs to be cleared and dedicated to its purpose. This work should be done with a light heart that is feeling the sacredness of the task. Make sure that the space only contains what contributes to the ceremony.

As well as a physical cleaning, it is important to include a way to clear out any heavy or sluggish spiritual energies that may be present in the space. Wafting smoke around the space from burning special plants such as sage or incense is one method. Sweet scents may also be used for the purpose of clearing. Spraying a room with light, lavender water or Agua de Florida[47] can be very useful, especially when burning something is not possible. For scent-sensitive individuals, using a spray bottle of purified water and a few drops of a scentless flower essence is a wonderful way to clear a space. Again, the feelings you hold and project from your body while engaging in the activity are paramount and outweigh the importance of the substances that you use.

Once cleared, it is important to program the space for the task to come. As I finish with a clearing, I envision—again in my feeling body—the action that is to happen. For instance, if the space is to be used for a wedding, I feel the couple lovingly embracing, happily moving through their lives together, and surrounded by those who love them. For the naming of a baby, I might feel the child growing up loved, secure, well, and strong. If the space is to be used for healing, I feel the client in perfect wholeness, already healed and vital. It is as though with this action of feeling it "already done" I am not only programming the space, but also alerting the helpful and healing spirits of what is about to unfold. That naturally leads me to the next element of ritual, which is the calling together of the spirits who will be participating in the ceremony.

Honoring the seen and unseen—calling together the participants. As I have stated before, your shaman powers come from learning how to be in *reverent participatory relationship* with All That Is. Attending to these relationships puts us in harmony with the flow of universal energies. Since we are connected to everything and all beings, we impact all of them with our choices and our actions. Everything we feel, think, and act upon creates ripples in the web, and our ceremonies happen within the context of this web, too. In the clearing and dedicating of space outlined in the previous paragraphs, we are communicating to the spirit community that we are about to engage in an activity. It is a form of being both courteous and respectful.

Similarly, it is important to be clear about whom you wish to participate in your ceremony. If the participants are physical human beings, then you send an invitation that includes a clear intent for the ritual. When they arrive, you honor them with gratitude for their presence and participation. Unseen guests require the same kind of attention. For example, we begin a ceremony, workshop, or healing by honoring the spirits of those who are both physically and not physically present. Using the format of the directions, we honor the spirits of the seasons, elements, our animal and plant companions, the forces of nature, the ancestors, our descendants, and so on. We welcome and honor only those that are beneficial while, at the same time, feeling a sense of harmony and balance filling the space. Our honoring is usually done with our voices and rattles, but can also be done with songs, flute, drumming, or some other method of generating harmonious vibrations that are coherent with your feelings. Of course, the same can be accomplished in total silence while spreading cornmeal around the perimeter of the space or by dancing throughout it. Whatever the method you choose to use, remember to focus on the feelings of honoring and welcoming the helpful and healing aspects of the divine to participate in the harmony and balance of the space.

Opening the ceremony. Once the setting is ready and all the participants are welcomed, it is important to officially open the ceremony. In a way, this element of the ceremony communicates clearly to all who are choosing to be with you that you are about to begin. Sometimes this can be as simple as asking all who are present to share a moment of breath. They may be asked to imagine that they are all breathing one single breath with many bodies; every being who has gathered for the ceremony becomes unified into a coalesced whole. After this the ceremony begins in earnest.

Directing the flow. As the ceremony proceeds, describe each step clearly to the participants. When doing a ceremony in the woods and away from other people, I am still clear about each step with the animals, birds, and spirits with whom I share the woods. I do this through my feelings and sometimes even softly aloud. I should mention here that I am a big proponent of vocalizing our prayers. The human voice is an immensely powerful tool. We have the capacity to create the physical world through our feeling vibrations, and when we couple those with actual vibrations from our voice, we magnify their effects.

Making closure. Just as a clear beginning is an important aspect of ceremony, so is a clear point of closure. Thank the nonphysical beings and let them know that your work together is done. Let yourself be filled with gratitude as you thank them for their participation, releasing them back into their normal flow. At this point, the physical humans who have gathered for the ceremony begin their return back to their ordinary lives. Honor them for their willingness to participate and share a snack or meal together. This helps them to ground back into their bodies so they are more able to *safely* engage in tasks like traveling home!

Now that you have some sense of the details that go into creating a ceremony, it is time to work with your spirit teacher to develop your way of actually doing it. Every shamanic practitioner has her or his own ways of working with the spirits, and it is important to find your own authentic way. What follows are journeys that can support you in getting clear information. After *each* journey, take the time to make notes in your journal and then make an offering of gratitude outside. It is best to work with each piece of information you receive prior to moving ahead. Remember, attend to the "Four I's" of living your life: *integrity* of purpose, words, and action; *integrating* the lessons that you are learning; *internalizing* the changes that you experience; and *implementing* the content of your journeys. The more you are able to do this, the more easily you will rely upon your spiritual connections in difficult situations, and the stronger a spirit walker you will become.

Journey Explorations

Journey with your power animal to your teacher to ask the following questions:

- "What is the best way for me to clarify my intent for ceremony?"

- "What is the best way for me to clear a space for ceremony?" or "What is my way to dedicate a space in which I will be performing ceremony?"

- "Along with my ceremony of honoring the directions, what is the best way for me to formally call together the participants in a ceremony?"

- "What is the best way for me to formally open a ceremony?"

- "How can I keep a ceremony flowing along in a way that honors the spirits, the participants, and the intent of the ceremony itself?"

- "What is the best way to close a ceremony?"

- "How can I support the participants to be safely grounded before they leave the ceremony?"

Communal Gratitude Offerings

While the offering rituals outlined in earlier chapters are quite simple, there are times in life when you may want to execute a more elaborate statement of gratitude: at special times such as holidays, the birth of a child, weddings, birthdays, or at the start or completion of a project. At these times, you want a celebratory gratitude ritual to include other people.

What follows are a series of communal gratitude rituals I have learned from my indigenous teachers and friends. After each one I provide you with journey questions about the ceremonies to clarify your intent and develop your own versions. In all cases, if you choose to perform ceremonies like these in your life, do remember to include all the above aspects. This will make for both powerful and safe experiences for you and your fellow participants.

Ulchi Offering Ceremonies

During my time with Grandfather Mikhail "Misha" Duvan, he taught us an offering ritual that was traditionally done to honor the Amur River. Before industrialization, the Ulchi culture was completely dependent upon the fish and fertility the river provided. To honor this vital connection, Grandfather Misha's people would make simple, small birch bark boats or bowls within which they would place a bit of rice, cookies, and fruit. The little boats would be placed on the water's surface to be carried away in the current. This flotilla of thankfulness floated downstream, feeding all the spirits of the river while thanking them for all that they provide. The river was fed twice a year—once when the ice was gone in April and again when the river began to freeze in November.

The traditional Ulchi practice their respect for the land spirits of place in a similar fashion by making ritualized offerings of food and vodka. This kind of ritual is called a *kaseegalee* or giving of thanks. In this ceremony, people honor the spirits of the world by literally feeding them and giving them drink. If being performed in the forest, this is done in front of the family's sacred larch tree[48] or *tudjia*. This tree functions like a personal family axis around which life revolves. As a representative of the World Tree, the *tudjia* telegraphs prayers throughout the three shamanic realms. Perhaps in recognition of these three worlds, the offerings begin with bowing three times.[49] After bowing, the spirit of the tree is fed vodka.[50] Making an offering of the vodka is done while holding the cup or glass in the left hand. The right middle (longest) finger is dipped into the vodka and then the liquid is flicked off the fingertip. In this way, it is the right or clean hand that actually makes the offering. First it is offered to the tree, then in the four directions as well as up and down to the Earth. This is all done from the same position so that the vodka is at times flicked over one's own shoulder. Then the cup is transferred to the right hand and a bit is poured out on the ground—pouring inward toward the left—to feed the spirits of the living forest. Then the person making the offering may drink a bit of the ceremonial vodka in communion with those spirits that have already been given drink.

Next the cup is put down and a small bowl of food is picked up in the left hand. The bowl contains the best kind of food and sweet treats, as well. The contents usually include rice, fruit, bread, nuts, dried fish, and candy.[51] The food is offered in small pinches with the right hand in the same order starting again with the tree first. As before, the last of the food is eaten by the person making the offering.

This form of offering is done very often. It is used to signal a change in action, a transition from one task to another and one time of year to another. Like other tribal, shamanic cultures, the Ulchi usually make their offerings before actions are taken. It is a way to thank the spirits prior to receiving anything, which is very different from how we approach offering gratitude in our culture. A *kaseegalee* is done before hunting or fishing or before entering the forest to fell trees to create a building. It may even be done to start a day. In the case of daily offerings, these may be made in the home at the altar called a *malee*—or sacred place in the southern part of a room.

In other rituals, the Ulchi ancestors would be fed in a similar manner. In their worldview, the ancestors made their lives possible, and although no longer in physical form, the ancestors' spirits were still very present. Ulchi families would create small wooden spirit houses to provide an honored place for them to live, containing small carvings of ancestral totems, personal talismans, and later on even photographs of deceased members of the family. Traditionally, these were placed in the family's personal larch tree. Later on, when village-centered life predominated and the forest was no longer the focus of spiritual life, the same spirit houses would be placed in the highest (cleanest) place in the family's home, which was usually up in the rafters.

On the first full moon in February, the living families' homes would be specially cleaned and prepared. At this point, their ancestors' spirit houses would be ceremonially placed in the center of the home near the hearth. Each family would then prepare special treats all day so that they could stay up all night to eat and celebrate with their ancestors. Once the preparations were complete, the spirit houses' entrance would be uncovered, prayers of gratitude for the gift of life would be offered to the ancestors, and the special food would be placed in ritual bowls. These bowls would then be placed in front of the entrance to the spirit house alongside of a cup of celebratory vodka. Once the ancestors had been fed, the family would share the meal to celebrate the life they had received from the ancestors—strengthening family bonds and insuring that the ancestors would continue to watch over the family.

Journey Explorations

Journey with your power animal to your teacher to ask the following questions. Do each one as a separate journey.

- "What is the best way for me to adapt the Ulchi water ceremony to honor the source of my drinking water?"
- "What is the best way for me to adapt the Ulchi ceremony for honoring the spirits of place around my home?"
- "What is the best way for me to create a 'house' for my ancestors in my home?"
- "What is the best way for me to adapt the Ulchi ceremony for honoring my ancestors?"
- "What is the right time of day and season for doing each of these ceremonies?"

Tuvan Fire Ceremony

Among the people of Central Asia, the offering of food and drink to honor the spirits is also widespread. The Tuvan traditional lifestyle on the lowland steppes involves herding sheep and horses across the vast, relatively treeless grassland of the Tuva republic and thus living in movable yurts made of heavy felt. A yurt's central fire is a survival essential for cooking, making tea, and keeping warm in Tuva's cold climate. As the central focus of nomadic living, the family's central fire becomes a living, breathing cosmic axis—a point of connection between sky and earth.

As the fire offers connection in this way, burning offerings is the method that is traditionally used to send prayers into the spirit world. Just as smoke travels through the smoke hole of the yurt and into the sky, so too can burned prayers or offerings travel into the upper realms of spirit.

When we sponsored Tuvan Ai Churek to come to Maine, she built a large fire and sang her gratitude to the fire as well as her spirit helpers. She then made an offering of the richest milk[52] and most prized parts of a cooked lamb to the roaring fire. Throughout the ceremony, she offered her gratitude to the spirit of the fire, the spirits of the sky who brought life-giving rain, the animals, the birds, the plants, and indeed, all of life. Upon completing her work of feeding the fire, she thanked the spirits for reciprocating and bestowing their blessings. In other words, she understood that just as she had offered nourishment to the spirits, they would naturally return the favor.

Journey Explorations

Embark on these journeys with your power animal to your teacher to learn how you may use a fire as a way to offer gratitude.

- "What is the best way for me to honor the spirits who support me through a fire ceremony?"
- "What times of the year are best for me to do this ceremony?"

A Nepalese Ceremony: The Kharga Puja

As a Nepalese *jhankri*, Bhola N. Banstola[53] does a few different kinds of ceremonies using a mandala drawn on a black cloth.[54] A mandala is a circular design that functions as an abstract diagram of the cosmos. It usually has several concentric levels that encompass the elements, the realms of spirit, and the levels of human consciousness or experience.

Several years ago, he shared a communal healing and thanksgiving ritual with a group of my students. The ritual is an opportunity for a group to release old wounds and heal relationships while receiving the blessings of a healing from the spirits. The ceremonial mandala became a safe container to hold the participants' unwanted energies and a doorway through which they could receive healing.

The black fabric on which the mandala is created represents the Universe. The color absorbs and encapsulates negative emotions. This gives them a place to reside away from the participants until a point when they are transmuted into harmless energy at the close of the ceremony.

During the ceremony a mixture of seven uncooked grains are used as an offering into the mandala. These can be any seven grains, and we typically use corn, quinoa, millet, white beans, black beans, orange peas, and yellow lentils. Rice is not in the mixture, as it is used alone as an offering substance on Bhola's altar.

Here is a key to the symbolism that Bhola draws on the cloth with finely ground corn flour that has been mixed with a bit of sacred red and yellow powdered pigments:

Figure 11. Nepalese ceremonial mandala.

Spirit Walking

The tridents. These represent the fire element that symbolizes the cosmic forces of transformation, change, and rebirth.

The three circles. The outer circle represents the Lower World, our body from the umbilicus down to our feet, our past and our birth in this lifetime. The second circle represents the Middle World, the center of the body from heart to umbilicus, the present time and our death or mortality. The inner ring represents the Upper World, the upper part of the body above the heart, the future time and our rebirth.

The four heads. These represent the four cardinal directions.

The four hands. These represent the cross-quarter directions.

The center of the mandala. The mandala's nine interior spaces are temporary houses for all the helpful spirits present for the ceremony. The central house is for the Sun and is honored with a bright yellow flower and a candle.

Once the drawing of the mandala is complete, the ceremonial leader speaks aloud the purpose for each round of the ceremony. After he has declared the focus for each round, each participant places a small handful of grain into the mandala while being filled with feelings of gratitude that the desired result has already been accomplished. Energetically, this creates a matrix into which reality will form itself. Our wounds and disturbances are absorbed by the mandala, and the offering confirms this.

There are nine rounds of offerings during the ceremony. The first seven provide opportunities to release physical, emotional, and spiritual maladies. The last two are to offer gratitude and welcome healing.

1. *The First Level of Transference and Healing.* This is focused on internal physical organs such as the heart, liver, kidneys, stomach, etc.

2. *The Second Level of Transference and Healing.* This level focuses on the external organs such as hair, nails, eyes, ears, and skin.

3. *The Third Level of Transference and Healing.* This level is focused on interpersonal relationships within the family.

4. *The Fourth Level of Transference and Healing.* This level focuses on healing the relationships at work and in the community.

5. *The Fifth Level of Transference and Healing.* This level focuses on bringing harmony and balance to the five elements that create our bodies and the Universe. At this level it is possible to work on environmental allergies or sensitivities and food allergies.

6. *The Sixth Level of Transference and Healing.* This level focuses on recognizing and diluting the emotions of past trauma, memories, anger, fear, sorrow, and suffering. This is an opportunity to disengage from your identity as a victim or wounded person.

7. *The Seventh Level of Transference and Healing.* This level focuses on realigning planetary problems that may be expressing themselves as issues of the body, mind, emotions, or spirit. The Nepalese people believe that the cosmos can impact our health and well-being. For this reason, attention is paid to supporting balance between Earth's neighbors as well as upon her surface.

8. *The Eighth Level of Transference and Healing.* The eighth level focuses on offering gratitude and thanksgiving to all the helpers, guides, ancestors, family, friends, and community that support us. We recognize that without our ancestors we

would not have life. Without our helping and guiding spirits, life would be a far more perilous journey.

9. *The Ninth Level of Transference and Healing.* The final level focuses on receiving blessings and grace. At this level, the participants visualize that they are receiving healing energy from the Universe in the form of golden rays of light entering their bodies and expanding out to All That Is. At this level of the ceremony the shaman sings songs of harmony, peace, tranquility, and longevity.

At the closing of the ceremony, the corners of the cloth are brought together, and the cloth is tied into a bundle with the grain held tightly inside. In this form, the bundle is traditionally carried to a flowing river or into the outgoing tide of the ocean and is placed into the water. Today, we simply open the bundle and release its contents into the moving water.

As the contents are released, give thanks in your heart for the spirits' blessings and the gift of having had a healing.

Journey Explorations

Take individual journeys to your teacher to ask the following questions:

- "What is the best way for me to perform the Nepalese ceremony of releasing wounds and receiving blessings safely?"
- "When is the best time for me to do this ceremony?"
- "What seven grains are my sacred grains?"

Andean Despachos

Another communal-style offering ceremony is the *despacho* of the Peruvian Andes. *Despachos* are beautiful bundles of flowers, food, sweets, small figures, shells, and other objects that are either burned or buried to deliver their gifts to the spirits. My group learned about creating *despachos* from our shaman friend, Fredy

"Puma" Quispe Singona,[55] who in turn had been taught by his grandfather Don Maximo Quispe. As I stated earlier, there is a belief among the peoples of the Andes in what they call *ayni*. This is usually translated to mean the state of *sacred reciprocity*—in other words, staying in harmony by giving to Mother Earth or *Pachamama* in order to create balance for all that we continue to be given. The *despacho* ceremony is a beautiful, elaborate, and communal way of creating this balance. In the *ayni despacho*, as with most traditional offering ceremonies, we give thanks *first*.

What follows here is a "North Americanized" version of an *ayni despacho*. It has been altered so that it uses substances that are more meaningful to us in this hemisphere and also more easily available. As you read through the instructions, you may wish to further tailor it to your region.

Figure 12. *Ayni despacho* foundation.

Exercise: Spirit Walker *Ayni Despacho* Ceremony

The *ayni despacho* is a good ceremony for times of transition, to give thanks for what is to come even more than for what has already passed. Your offerings are of what is considered to be the best because that's what you want to get back in the wheel of reciprocity.

Don Maximo, Puma Quispe Singona's grandfather and teacher, always taught that we must "first put your heart in the *despacho*"—by that he meant that we have to have genuine feelings of love and gratitude in our hearts when we begin. He also says, the "last *despacho* is the first"—in other words, create each and every ritual with fresh eyes and heart. Don't let the elements of ceremony become rote or stale.

Figure 13. Peruvian paqo, Fredy "Puma" Quispe Singona. Pen and ink.

Before you start the *despacho*, prepare where it will be placed. If you are planning to bury the offering, dig the hole. Bless the hole with cornmeal, perfume, and alcohol asking Pachamama to receive the offering into her body. If the *despacho* is going to be burned, build the structure of your fire but don't light it. Again, prepare the ground under the firewood with cornmeal, perfume, and alcohol to honor the fire for taking your prayers.

Since we are adapting our *despacho* ceremony to more closely reflect the spirits and resources of the North American continent, all of the offerings presented below are suggestions. If you do not have the exact ingredient, use your imagination to draw the object or use a magazine photo. The important thing is to pray from your heart and remember that whatever you include will be getting burned or buried in the end.[56]

1. Gather together in a circle. Everyone in the circle gets perfumed water poured into her or his hands. Participants then clap their hands together three times and inhale the scent to wake up the spirit. Pass your scented hands over your body head first and down to the floor. This combs away any heavy energy or *hucha* you may be carrying down and into Mother Earth. This is a way to intentionally release negativity so that Mother Earth can transmute it into usable, nourishing energy to support life.

2. Lay down your base. This is usually a sheet of sturdy, white paper. This paper functions as the envelope in which you send your prayers and dreams. Fold the paper three times vertically and three times horizontally, then unfold it. The resulting nine squares create a central square in which you will build the *despacho*.

3. Next, create the base of flowers. Place red flowers around the edge of the central square, creating a border. Carnations work wonderfully well for this ceremony. Red flowers represent Pachamama, she who provides our physical existence—our food, air, water, and our actual bodies. Dismember the red flowers by carefully twisting the petals from the green base from which they emerge. Lay the blossoms so that they fall open around the edge of the central square with deep thanks for all Mother Earth's gifts.

Figure 14. A lead charm used in traditional Peruvian *despachos*.

4. Once this is complete, fill the center of this red border with white flowers that you prepare as you did the red ones. White flowers represent the *Apus*, or spirits of place, the dominant spirits in the area, what's closest to your heart in the local area, on your home ground. As you fill in the square with the white flowers, give with thanks for places from which you source your power. The flowers create the base to cradle your offerings in the same manner as Pachamama and the *Apus* cradle all of us. Sprinkle sugar over this base to sweeten the offering. Add more sugar over the *despacho* as it is being built.

5. The center of the offering is a scallop shell which represents the womb of Pachamama—the source of all life. Place inside the shell one black, red, yellow, white, and brown bean. We use different

color beans to represent the different colors of humanity—male/female, young/old. Speak your honoring prayers—out loud—as you go along.

6. Above this center create a sky. Make clouds of cotton balls and use colored thread to construct a rainbow. To represent the Sun and Moon, use silver and gold foil or paper cutouts. The Moon (silver) is placed on the left; the Sun (gold) is placed on the right. Place the objects in a clockwise fashion and don't separate Earth and sky. Let the rainbow tie them together. Sprinkle paper stars over the entire *despacho* to represent our stellar brothers and sisters. This reminds us of the gifts we received when supernovas created all of the elemental building blocks necessary for life.

7. Continue to build the *despacho*. Place a starfish to represent the angelic or enlightened ones—spiritual beings that come to us in our journeys. Add a cross to represent and honor the four cardinal directions.

8. Don't forget to keep adding more sugar so that life will be sweet!

9. Now add things that represent what you are thankful for in your world. These things can be made of paper or of shaped cookies or candy—use your imagination! Add incense and sage for perfume in life and spiral shells to remind us that life is a spiral path.

Beans, squash seeds, and corn are thought of in North America as the Three Sisters of the First People. Since they grow best when planted together, they represent the power of community and that fact that we function best when we work together. Rice is added to the *despacho* as a symbol of wealth, as it is a grain that must be purchased by Andean people. Animal crackers represent all the animals on which we depend and who share our world. Alphabet noodles represent the sacred, magical words of ritual, words of prayer, of love, and those used in storytelling. Candy and confetti are sprinkled throughout to offer thanks and to ask for beauty in life. We add crystals for clarity, and a lodestone, as well. This is a natural magnet that is used to draw abundance and make our prayers "attractive!"

Use something to represent your ancestors. Small photocopied images of a cherished family photo are great for this. Instead of the traditional llama fat, add butter for richness and a hollow eggshell with its contents removed to represent your unborn dreams, beginning relationships, and projects that haven't yet hatched. Also add a sprinkling of alcohol for celebration. A lit candle in the center celebrates light and the element of Fire, while play money is used to represent the abundance that we require to live well.

If there is something personally special that you wish to give thanks for, make a drawing to represent it and add it to the *despacho*.

This is the foundation for your prayers that will be placed in the offering in the form of a *k'intu*.

10. Now everyone who participates makes a three-leaf *k'intu*. While the Peruvians use three coca leaves, you can use the more readily available bay leaves. Remember, it's the intent of the prayer and the ceremony itself that count. Each person holds the leaves like a fan with the stems pointing down and breathes their heartfelt prayers into it. They give thanks for the good things in their lives that they want to continue and those they would like to have happen— speaking them out loud, from the heart while feeling their prayers already answered. All celebrants let their breath carry their feelings into the *k'intu*.

While the participants are breathing their prayers into the leaves and saying them aloud, make one two-leaf *k'intu* for the *Apus* and one three-leaf *k'intu* for Pachamama. Place them in the *despacho* as anchors for all of the other individual prayers. With this gesture, you are also reminding yourself that Pachamama and the *Apus* have prayers/dreams of their own.

11. Each *k'intu* is placed on the foundation and sprinkled with confetti, alcohol, and sugar.

12. At this juncture the people of the Andes would share red wine and pisco or other white spirits like rum. Of course, you can also use red juice or soda for Pachamama and a clear drink for the *Apus*. Breathe thanks onto the glasses, say "Salute," and drink up. If possible and if your location allows for you to do so, pour some of each beverage onto the ground for the elementals and helpful/healing spirits.

13. Now, fold up the *despacho* bundle, bottom up, top down, right in, left in. Tie the bundle very tightly with red string or yarn while keeping it upright. Tuck a flower into the knot to decorate the bundle.

14. The completed *despacho* bundle may now be used to heal those present. While praying to the spirits, run the *despacho* down each person's body, from the head to the feet, both front and back. When you get to the feet of the person, actually touch the ground at the end of the pass down the body. This gives the heavy energy or *hucha* to Pachamama to use as an energetic fertilizer.

15. When you are done with every person, place the *despacho* bundle in the prepared hole or light your fire and burn the bundle while holding gratitude in your heart.

Figure 15. *Despachos* **may be created with many different beautiful and sweet ingredients.**

Journey Explorations

As with the other ceremonies, it is important to take journeys to learn how to make this ritual your own.

- "What is the best way for me to perform the *ayni despacho* ceremony?"

- "What ingredients are important to include in my *ayni despacho* ceremony?"

- "Under what circumstances is it useful for me to perform an *ayni despacho* ceremony?"

- "When are the best times for me to do this ceremony?"

Process Questions

- Articulate, as best as you can, in your journal the bodily, emotional, and spiritual sensations of performing a group gratitude ritual.

- How does it differ from doing your individual gratitude ritual?

- Think about how these practices could benefit your family or community.

Making Ceremonies Your Own

Every shamanic culture has some form of communal ritual to unite a group of people for the purpose of honoring the spirits. While borrowing one of these rituals is acceptable, it would be far more beneficial to work with your spirits to find rituals that would be relevant to your own life and cultural experience. If you choose to duplicate these rituals in your life, do remember to include all the aspects of ceremony I have outlined. This will make for both powerful and safe experiences for you and your fellow participants. Remember to eat and chat together after your ceremony or ritual. You want to support the people who attend your event as they safely ground back into ordinary reality.

Chapter 18

The Voice as Shaman's Tool

he ability to speak is uniquely human, and the human voice is our oldest healing instrument. It has an amazing capacity for delivering energy, and when used in an intentional way, your voice may enhance your connection to power, give an offering to the spirits, impart blessings, deliver healing, soothe, energize, and positively shift the spiritual atmosphere in a place. When used in a negative or unintentional manner, a voice can also do harm. Anyone who has been verbally abused by another person can attest to its power to wound.

Many of the clients we see in our practice are working to heal from the negative perceptions they hold. Often the roots of these terrible misperceptions are the negative messages they received in early childhood. You see, when people speak around or to children in a cruel, belittling, or abusive manner, the children internalize the energy of these messages since in early childhood the part of our brains that can discern the self from the surroundings hasn't yet developed.

Indeed, when we are children—particularly in our own preverbal developmental phase—the communications we hear (and see) around us become part of our worldview or paradigm of life. In essence, these communications create a fabric of reality. So if you grow up in an atmosphere of loving words and clear, kind actions, you will develop a stronger belief in the inherent "goodness" of yourself and the world at large. On the other hand, if the surroundings you were in were chaotic or abusive, you may have learned that you were "bad" and the world was a threatening place. These harmful effects are amplified when negative speech is directed toward the child.

Our child within is always present. He or she is part of our subconscious and is always listening. The messages we hear as we continue through adulthood have the effect of either reinforcing the negative messages we heard as children or healing them. It is not only the communication we hear from others that can have this impact; the way we speak to and about ourselves is also important. For this reason, shamans learn to use their voice mindfully and choose their words with care. A spirit walker knows that each exchange of speech has the energetic potential for healing or harm.

Exercise: Observing Speech

Much of the vocalizations human beings engage in are unintentional. People are generally not mindful about their speech and unclear in their communications. Test this out by engaging in what I like to call "loving anthropological observation" of the people with whom you are in contact. Listen to them speaking to each other and notice how they speak. Please do this exercise with compassion and without calling the other person's attention to what you notice.

Observe how the people around you speak to each other and refer to themselves.

- Do they choose their words thoughtfully?
- How do they use language?
- Do they diminish another or themselves through the way they speak?
- Are they reinforcing positive or negative perceptions about the world and themselves?

Also notice how much of their speech is filled with verbal interruptions or pause fillers such as "um," "like," or "uh." These unintentional expressions have the effect of distracting the listener and diluting the communication, thereby diminishing the potential transfer of energetic information.

Now observe yourself! This is best done with a recording device. Again, with compassion, just record a typical, relaxed conversation.

- How do you use language?
- Are you directing negative statements toward yourself or others?
- Do you use verbal interruptions in your speech?

Record what you have observed in your notebook.

Shamanic Singing and Chanting

For the shaman, besides calling helpful and healing spirits, raising your voice through singing or chanting can have a similar effect as drumming or rattling. In his paper, "Trance States: A Theoretical Model and Cross-Cultural Analysis,"[57] Michael Winkelman asserts: "Trance states associated with magico-religious practices are based on varied manipulations of the organism, all of which lead to a parasympathetic dominant state characterized by the dominance of the frontal cortex by slow wave discharges emanating from the limbic system."[58] "Rhythmic auditory stimulation imposes a pattern upon the brain that is distinct from the normal asynchronous pattern."[59] In other words, this shift in brain pattern is consistent with the shamanic state of consciousness.[60] Winkelman suggests that there are various methods that produce this state of being, including drumming, rattling, and chanting.

For many people, the act of singing or even speaking up can be difficult: They many have been told that they "couldn't carry a note." For others the trauma of their early life created a need for "invisibility" which led to silence. For still others there is the belief that what they have to say (or sing) will not be received by others.

Overcoming these old obstructions to your voice can be a challenge; however, it is a necessary part of being a spirit walker. Since chanting has the capacity to expand your awareness, it is another "tool" the wise spirit walker cultivates.

Let me reassure you that your voice is already remarkable. You can speak, cry, shout, laugh, and sing because of the amazing equipment with which you were born. Based on fossil evidence, the human voice we know today may have evolved in ancestors who lived more than fifty thousand years ago.[61] In other words, not only is your voice a natural part of your being, it has had thousands of years of refinement behind it.

What follows is an easy exercise to begin the process of opening up your voice. It is a simple one-syllable chant that may be done like an audible sigh. Chanting in this form is something anyone can accomplish easily without any training.

Exercise: A Simple Chant

Sit with your back straight and your feet on the floor or ground for this exercise. Have a timer nearby which you can easily set for thirty minutes. You will be chanting the heart sound "ah."

1. Close your eyes and breathe in a calm, restful manner.
2. Once you feel centered, tone the syllable "ah" as you exhale.
3. Do not concern yourself with achieving a specific note or tone.
4. Sing whatever note feels easiest for your voice.
5. Once you feel comfortable, start the timer.
6. Repeat toning on every exhalation.
7. Continue toning in this fashion for the whole thirty minutes.
8. At the end, gently allow yourself to come back to ordinary awareness and record your experience as you have done in prior exercises. You may have noticed a shift in awareness happening while you were toning. Record whatever you noticed in your journal.

The syllable "ah" is known as the primordial vowel sound of the Sanskrit and Tibetan alphabets. It is the seed of all other sacred sounds. When chanted repeatedly, it has the effect of smoothing out energy, calming the mind, and allowing the body to deeply relax. In this way, it can be thought of like a deep sigh! If you feel ungrounded after this or any other exercise, please do the Embodied Light meditation exercise and follow it with an offering and spending some time outdoors.

Figure 16. Nepalese *jhankri* Bhola Nath Banstola preparing for a ceremony. Photo.

Different Kinds of Shamanic Song

Our friend Bhola provides an excellent example of using the voice as a shamanic tool. All parts of his shamanic practice have a "soundtrack" that helps him to call, access, and harness the powers that are necessary to heal. Bhola begins to sing when he first gets ready to shamanize.

As he is preparing his costume, drum, and other tools, he sings specific songs to awaken these objects for their work. A shaman sings to and with the sacred objects as they have become living partners with whom the shaman *collaborates* in the same manner as he does with other beneficial spirits.

Once Bhola is dressed and ready to begin, he sings to create a sacred space within which he will do his work, and he raises power by singing his songs of power which call the spirits who will guide him. As he works with a patient, he may sing a healing song, one to exorcise unbeneficial energy, a song to coax a person's soul back into the body, or a song to discover hidden information. Finally, when he has completed his work, he sings to send the helping spirits back to their realms in celebration and gratitude and to put all his shamanic accoutrements back to sleep.

Through my own experience of shamanic practice and studying the work of other shamans, I have come up with this simplified list of how song may be used.

Shamans have songs to

- Call the spirits, including declarations of intent and creating sacred space
- Awaken the spirits of sacred objects
- Raise the shaman's personal power, which includes merging with protective spirits
- Release unbeneficial spiritual energy from a person, place, or object
- Return beneficial spiritual energy to a person, place, or object

- Work directly on a patient's body/mind/spirit to relax them and allow deeper healing
- Welcome in a soul at birth
- Sing a soul out of this world at death
- Work with the weather
- Heal the land
- Offer gratitude to the helpful, healing spirits who have assisted in the shaman's work
- End the work (release the shaman's spirit helpers, put the sacred objects back to sleep, close the space, and return the shaman to an ordinary way of being)
- Do many, many other things!

As you can see, developing a strong vocal practice is essential to being a shaman. Along with your power song, you will discover many fresh, spirit songs for your practice. These won't be songs that have been written down or sung before. Instead, they are songs that you will get directly from the spirits. You will learn them over time and through the deepening of the relationships you have with your helpful spirits. Here are a few journeys that can be of assistance to you in growing your powers of shamanic song. Do not try to do them all at once! Instead, allow a few weeks or so between them so that you can fully internalize each of the songs.

Exercise: A Journey to Find an Honoring Song

- Journey to ask your power animal, "What is the song I sing to honor you?"

Immediately upon returning from the journey, sing this song for half an hour to fully internalize it. Once you are finished singing, you can write your notes and observations. After making notes, remember to make an offering to the spirits. Since the voice and the element of Air are so intimately related, speak out loud as you make your offering. You may also wish to toss cornmeal into the breeze, burn incense, shake a rattle, or ring a small bell to accompany your voice.

Exercise: Journeys to Find Other Songs

- Journey to ask your power animal, "How do I access your powers through singing?"

- Journey to ask your primary spirit teacher, "What is the song I sing to honor you?"

- Journey to ask your primary spirit teacher, "How do I access your powers through singing?"

- Take other journeys to your power animal or primary spirit teacher to ask, "What song/chant can heal my body?" or "What chant/ song can help heal another person?"

- In separate journeys, ask your power animal or primary spirit teacher to take you to the spirit of your drum, your rattle, your staff, and any other shamanic sacred objects[62] you use to ask, "What is your song?"

Remember to immediately sing each song for half an hour to fully internalize it. Once you are finished singing, write your notes and observations. After making notes, remember to make an offering to the spirits. Since the voice and the element of Air are so intimately related, speak out loud as you make your offering. You may also wish to toss cornmeal into the breeze, burn incense, shake a rattle, or ring a small bell to accompany your voice.

Overtone Singing

Overtone singing, also known as throat singing, overtone chanting, or harmonic singing, is a type of vocalization in which additional harmonic resonances are created along with a droning, fundamental tone. In some cases, multiple resonances may be produced simultaneously. Unlike notes sung in a normal fashion, these overtone harmonics are pure in that they are usually one single pitch, whereas typically a sung tone has a variation of vibrations present. This gives the overtone harmonics a clear, bell-like, or flutelike sound.

This kind of singing has been popularized through the spread of Tibetan Buddhist rituals, performances of groups from the republic of Tuva, and recordings and film soundtracks. Karlheinz Stockhausen was one of the first Western composers to use this kind of sound in his vocal piece *Stimmung* in 1968.[63]

As with other shamanic vocal styles such as *joiking*, overtone chanting has a quality of mimicry. The sounds are very akin to what you hear in nature: the birds, flowing water, the wind, and animal sounds are often incorporated into overtone chanting when used by the shaman. According to Boric Petrovic in his article "Overtone Singing/Throat Singing,"[64] "*khoomei* (a specific form of Tuvan throat singing) is an integral part in the ancient pastoral animism that is still practiced today." Petrovic continues, "the animistic world view of this region identifies the spirituality of objects in nature, not just in their shape or location, but in their sound as well." He further adds that "human mimicry of nature's sounds is seen as the root of throat singing." In other words, this form of singing was firmly in place prior to the arrival of Buddhism in Central Asia and has its roots in the shamanic past.

~~~~~~

Exercise: Learning to Overtone Sing

This kind of sound-making is accomplished by changing the shape of the tongue, lips, throat, or nasal passages to create new, complex resonances to accompany a basic sung tone. A good way to begin is to sing the sound "errr" and touch your tongue to the roof of your mouth. Now fool around a bit with the position of your tongue by sliding it farther back or forward while gradually making an "oo" shape with your lips.

As you continue this, you will begin to hear a whistle-like second tone being produced. As you practice, you may find that by keeping a single fundamental note and changing the shape of your mouth, you can make an overtone melody.

The sounds produced in this fashion are somewhat "otherworldly," and singing in this way can be a wonderfully meditative activity. I love to overtone sing as a part of my shamanic powering up ritual. I usually start with singing my power song, then flow into other songs given to me by Spirit and intersperse overtone chanting throughout. The transcendent Middle World beings—whom I will introduce later in this book—as well as the animals and bird spirits with whom I work, are particularly fond of these sounds.[65]

There are many good sources for learning overtone chanting/throat singing both online and in book form. If you are called to play with sound this way in your shamanic practice, I highly recommend the teachings of Jill Purce from the UK and actually listening to examples by Siberian or Central Asian vocal groups. In addition, it is important to practice outside in nature. As you would do with any of the shamanic lessons in this book, create a clear intent and practice in a respectful, loving way.

Process Questions

- Articulate, as best as you can, in your journal the bodily, emotional, and spiritual sensations of using your voice in new ways.

- How do these sensations differ from the way that you previously felt about your voice?

- Think about how using your voice could benefit your shamanic practice. Record your impressions.

Chapter 19

Divination: Other Ways of Exploring the Invisible Worlds

Divination is another method a little different than journeying which spirit walkers use to access the spirit world to address practical life issues: unraveling a problem, accessing a different perspective, coming to grips with a life change, or living our lives in greater harmony.

As you already have learned, the world of the shaman extends beyond the consensual reality of ordinary time and space. In the shamanic realms, all time happens at once and all space is still unified. When shamans access the world beyond, they are able to perceive that which has not yet occurred in ordinary reality. This is important, as information that is hidden from us by space or time might be what is needed to implement a shift in the self, reveal a truth, or offer keys to making life decisions. It is not so much that the spirit walker is able to see into the future, but that the spirit world exists beyond and before form itself manifests. In that realm, neither matter nor time is yet fixed. All is still in flux and flow. It is where many potential possibilities are waiting to be made physical.

There are several general categories of divinatory methods typically used by shamans. These include *spontaneous prophesy*, including dreaming and spontaneous visions; *augury*, interpreting signs found in nature or patterns in objects; and *sortileges*, the casting or drawing of objects and various forms of dowsing. In practice, categories become blurred. For instance, when shamans cast objects for divination, they also may interpret the patterns and information the objects provide or rely upon the spontaneous information the spirits provide during the reading.

While you may be more familiar with divinatory cards, such as the tarot, dowsing, or the casting rune stones, the art of shamanic divination may be performed in a myriad of different ways. As shamans perform divinatory functions for their communities, they may use objects like pebbles, grain, crystals, and bones to foretell future events or unravel the mysteries of the present.

In many parts of southern Africa, the *sangoma* or "witch doctor" shaman might use an entire collection of objects to provide spiritual information. Similar methods are found in the Amazon basin. In either case, a complex array of bones, seeds, teeth, beads, stones, claws, sticks, and the like are cast together. Sometimes, as in the Amazonian traditions, the special painted surface on which the objects are thrown provides an even deeper level of context for the objects themselves.

Specially inscribed bones, wood, or ivory pieces may be thrown like dice to provide the patterns for the diviner to interpret. As such, this method has similarities to casting runes, in that the diviner reads both patterns as well as the content drawn on the objects themselves.

While these methods are quite complex, many shamans use simpler means for the same results. For instance, Bhola uses a small pinch of uncooked rice that he tosses on a drumhead. From the patterns of the rice and numbers of grains in sections of those patterns, he is able to receive information about a person's circumstance. This is somewhat similar to the Tuvan small white pebbles or the *paqo* bundle of loose coca leaves tossed onto a cloth.

Osteomancy, or the use of animal bones for divination, is found in many different cultures across the world. For instance, *scapulimancy*[66] is the art of reading patterns in the shoulder bone of a sheep, goat, deer, or caribou to determine the spirits' will.

This practice is remarkably widespread from ancient civilizations in China, Central Asia, Greece, and northern Europe to communities of North American indigenous peoples.

Even the drum itself can be used as a divination tool. In the Sami traditions of the European arctic, the shaman's drum has many symbols depicting the spirit world painted across its face. To perform divination, a small pointer, which may be a piece of reindeer antler or another object is placed upon the drum face. The drum is then gently beaten as the shaman sings a journey. Where the pointer lands provides additional guidance.

In other places an entire animal, typically one raised for food, may be used to divine hidden knowledge. For instance, in Peru the entrails of a guinea pig may be read to determine the nature of a person's spiritual illness or provide support about choosing a direction in which to proceed at a crossroad in one's life.

For myself, I find that divination to be a combination of reading what the objects I'm using are revealing while directly receiving information from the spirits. Therefore, to accomplish divination, it is best to be in the shamanic state of consciousness. This allows the spirits of the objects to share their wisdom and other spirits that you trust to elaborate with more detail.

Exercise: Divination with Natural Objects

All elements of the natural world have a spirit, and as such, everything around you in nature may be a support for you when a question arises in your heart. Rocks, a gnarled piece of driftwood, the bark of a tree, weathered seashells, and the patterns of clouds are all spirits that can be tapped for guidance through divination.

1. Begin by framing a question as you would for a journey. While holding that question in mind, go out onto the land to look for a larger stone, a piece of wood, or another object that stands out, "speaks to you," or presents itself.

2. Now set the object down and let your question go. Look into the surface of the object without moving it and see what images arise. Allow the shapes and patterns of the object's texture to become images. This is a bit like seeing animals in the clouds on a summer's day or taking a Rorschach test. Without thinking about the images, simply write them down.

3. Once you have four to six images, think about each image and ask yourself what it means to you. Take the first thing that comes to your mind and write that meaning down as well.

4. Take the separate meanings that struck your for each image and create a kind of summary of what these are saying to you.

When you have finished, take the object back to where you found it and place an offering on the land in gratitude to it and its surroundings. I find that this method is a great way to get out of the way when journeys on a topic start feeling vague or baffling. Nature always provides me with very grounded, strong information that is fresh and helps to clarify my mind on whatever subject has me in turmoil or confusion.

Exercise: Working with a Divination Bundle

Once you have gotten comfortable using one object for divination, you may want to expand your repertoire. As I stated earlier, many shamans use an assembly of sacred objects for divinatory work. These may have been given to the spirit walker by her or his mentor, passed down from an ancestor, or found as gifts from the spirits. There may be dozens of objects in the bundle, each with layers of meaning that are then shaded by their relationship with others in the casting and by the ground on which they are cast. While it can take a lifetime to truly master the complex ways this method can express itself, it is possible to begin making and using a simple divination bundle.

1. When you feel ready to embark upon this work, take time to center yourself, make an offering, and then power up by connecting with your helping spirits and singing your power song. Merge with your

teacher or power animal, and then go out into nature to gather a few small durable objects like acorns, small pebbles, shells, etc. Use what nature provides. When you have your objects, unmerge from your tutelary spirit and bring the objects back to your home. Place the things you have gathered on your altar.

2. Do a journey to ask if anything else you have might be useful in the bundle. For instance you may have a sacred stone, animal claw, or such that may want to be included. Collect those things and place them alongside the objects you gathered in nature and leave them all on your altar for three days. While you wait, you may write down a bit about your experience and anything of importance that you learned in the process.

3. On the fourth day, journey to your teacher or power animal again and have him or her empower the things that you have gathered together on your altar for your divination bundle. Ask the spirits to imbue the objects with sacred wisdom.

Figure 17. A divination bundle may include objects such as bones, stones, acorns, coins, beads, and other objects. Photo.

Divination: Other Ways of Exploring the Invisible Worlds

4. When the spirits are through with their work, spend some time rattling or drumming with the objects for a while. When you have connected with them, place the objects into their own special container. This can be a cloth bag or another container you have dedicated for this purpose. Also select a cloth that will be the sacred space for your readings and onto which the objects will be cast.

5. When you feel ready, formulate a question or have a friend come with a question so that you may begin using the bundle.

6. Once a question is clear, merge with your teacher, and then "cast" the objects by pouring the objects down onto the cloth. Use your enhanced, shamanic sight as well as your intuition to read the messages presented by your divination bundle.

Fire Gazing

Among the Huichol people of Mexico, the spirit of fire is a powerful teacher. The sacred fire is what the Huichol believe enables them to experience visions. You, too, can work with the spirit of fire for the purposes of divining wisdom. To work with a powerful elemental such as Fire, it is important to be impeccable with your intentions and actions. For this reason, do the following journeys to prepare for the work.

Journey Questions

- Journey to a teacher or power animal to ask them: "How may I work safely with fire for divination?"

- Also ask: "Please teach me the song to safely work with fire."

Record the content of your journey and practice the song until you have it memorized. Make an offering upon your return.

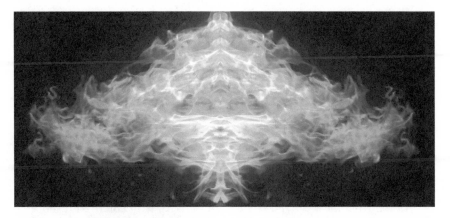

Figure 18. Fire Being. Digital art.

Once you have completed the journeys and have gained some measure of understanding of working with fire, you are ready to begin. Set aside a time to do the work. Night is the very best for working with the fire as its illumination is most profound in darkness.

Exercise: Working with Fire

Prepare yourself by cleansing yourself and the location where the fire is to be prepared as you might for a special time with a treasured loved one. Once physically clean, honor the spirits of all directions and ask them to bless the area where you will be working. You may also use an aromatic substance to "sweeten" the air of the area.

Then, gather all your preparatory materials such as your drum and rattle, your other sacred tools, and all the firewood and kindling you will need. Do this in a mindful manner with the purpose of the ceremony held in your heart. Keep safety in mind at all times as you are working, and if you are going to build a fire outdoors, have a bucket of water on hand to quench any errant sparks.

1. Once all has been gathered, make an offering in the fireplace or on the ground in the fire ring that will receive the fire. Thank the place for holding the fire for you. I use perfume and cornmeal or cedar sprigs for this purpose. However, you may use whatever you normally use for an offering.

2. Now set up a small fire but do not light it yet. Once the kindling and firewood are ready to receive the match, begin rattling softly and singing the fire song you learned from your teacher.

3. Let the fire know that you have a question and are seeking its wisdom. Then light the fire. As the wood begins to catch, sing more loudly with the intent of honoring the fire spirit with your song. To show gratitude to the fire spirit for working with you, toss a small bit of offering material into the flames to feed it.

4. When the fire is full, sit as close to it as you can safely, and ask your question aloud from your heart. Rattle softly and gaze deeply into the fire. Allow the fire spirit to give you its wisdom. You may see images in the flames or you may hear its voice whisper to you. The fire will communicate to your heart in its own way. As the fire dies to coals, it will continue to provide insight, so it is important to stay with the fire until it completely goes out. As the embers cool, you may journal the insights that you have received.

5. When through, make an offering to the spirits for their loving assistance.

On the next morning when you are sure the last of the coals are completely cold, take a bit of the ashes and mix them with cornmeal or flour to sprinkle on the earth. Again thank the fire, the air, the wood, and earth for their gifts.

Process Questions

After you have practiced divination by using elements from the natural world, notice how your connection to spirit and nature has shifted. After some practice, ask yourself these questions and record what you realize about your own process.

- How does being able to receive information from the divination bundle alter your experience of the objects?

- What was your experience of working with a fire to gain insight?

Chapter 20

The Spiritual Population of the Middle World

A *spirit walker must cultivate* strong relationship bonds in the Middle World. These connections not only include those with the spirits of the birds, plants, animals, and various landscape features, they also include the ancient "spirit people" or transcendent nature beings. These spirits are the ones that stand between the physical and nonphysical worlds. They collaborate in the process of manifestation, and their presence on the land indicates that an area is spiritually healthy.

You may have noticed how plots of land feel different from each other—even when they look very similar. Some may feel empty and hollow while others nearly sizzle with enlivening energy. What creates these different feelings is the spiritual health of the land. When a place becomes overused, or the human beings living on it fall out of right relationship with it, the transcendent spirits may begin to recede. When these spirits withdraw their enlivening energies, a landscape begins to feel barren and deadened. Just as you choose when and with whom you engage based upon how well you are treated, the transcendent spirits of the Middle World have similar discernment about when and where they reside. A shaman's role has always included being in harmonious relationship with these spirits, so that the land and the beings that depend upon it remain healthy.

Your growing practice of gratitude and studying nature in your square yard has prepared you for connecting with and stepping into relationship with the natural world. As I stated earlier, this emotional and spiritual bond to nature is critical for anyone wanting to follow the shamanic path. No matter where we live, the complex, interdependent web of the biosphere nourishes and sustains our physical existence. Spirit walkers contribute to keeping it healthy and inspirited.

The transcendent nature spirits straddle the line between the ordinary and non-ordinary worlds. Previous generations who lived much closer to the land than most of us do today told stories about these spirits, sang songs about them, and even carved their faces into cathedrals. To our ancestors, these spirits were as real as you or I. They are the fairies, green men/green women, giants, pixies, elves, sprites, nymphs, gnomes, brownies, mermaids/mermen, and so on. These spirits embody Wild Nature, the untamed and regenerative force that produces the robust and essential aliveness expressed in healthy organisms and bioregions. Through relationship with these spirits, you can reweave your own connections to Wild Nature, which contribute to restoring the place where you live.

Our ancestors often knew these spirits very well. For example, my Norwegian immigrant grandmother occasionally put a saucer of milk and a bowl of oatmeal out on her porch, even into the 1970s. She was not feeding the neighborhood cat, but rather doing as her parents and grandparents on the farm had done. She was giving a treat to the *nisse*,[67] gnome-like, indigenous nature spirits.

These *nisse* are also known as *vörðr*, a word that comes from Old Norse meaning a caretaker, warden, or watcher. These are designations common to other transcendent nature spirits as well. For the Old Norse, the *nisse* or *vörðr* were thought of as the original watchers or guardians of the land. This designation was also used for very old trees—most often a linden, elm, or ash—under which these spirits were thought to dwell. All *nisse* don't live on the land, however. The seafaring Norse honored those that chose to take up residence aboard their ships as the *skibsnisse* or ship gnomes.

Wherever they resided, these beings were honored and respected. Since the *nisse* were an older race and had closer and deeper connections with nature, they could function like intermediaries on behalf of the humans with whom they were in relationship— just as you might help out a good and treasured friend. This understanding was passed from generation to generation, and Norse folktales still contain stories of the hapless characters who found their milk pails overturned, their cows' tails tied together, and their fishing nets empty when they, through their poor relationships with the *nisse,* lost the favor of these spirits.

Appearance of Middle World Spirits

In my experience, many of the transcendent Middle World nature spirits have a hybridized or altered humanlike form. These beings often appear as having both human aspects as well as aspects of their form that look as though they were borrowed from a plant, animal, bird, insect, or other part of nature. The sorcerer painted on the cave of Trois Frères is an excellent example of this hybridized form that dates to the Upper Paleolithic time in Europe. He is an upright, dancing figure of a man with the antlered head and tail of a deer.

The Green Man offers another excellent example of this hybridized appearance. He has a shaggy, foliated head—part human and part growing plants. He represents many interrelated energies. For instance, his face can remind us of the irrepressibility of life, the immutable force that allows grass to squeeze its way between the cracks in a sidewalk, tree roots to heave up city paving or split a stone, and a weed's stubborn ability to demand its place in an orderly garden.

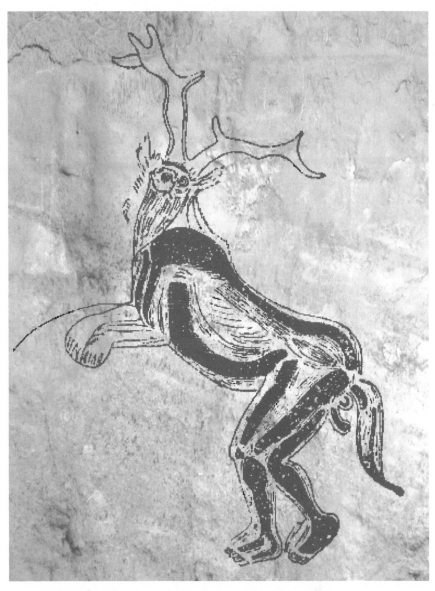

Figure 19. The Shaman of Trois Frères. Digital image.

He also stands as a consort of and partner with the Earth Goddess. As the son and lover of the Great Mother, he is destined to regenerate every spring to watch over her fruitfulness and recede into darkness once again when she takes her winter slumber. The Green Man's circle of death and resurrection reminds us of the cyclic rhythms of the world that are paradoxically both eternal and transitory. Life will reassert itself, even as individual beings die.[68]

Figure 20. The Green Man. Acrylic on rag illustration board.

By guarding our green relations—those who give us our breath and the stable foundation for the planet's food chain—the Green Man supports the continuance of all of nature.[69]

Spirits who function in this role are sometimes depicted as shape-shifters caught in a state of partial metamorphosis. Standing with one foot in the spirit world and one foot in ordinary reality, it is as though they are in the doorway—giving ordinary human beings a way to interact with the mysteries of life. These spirits mirror the spirit walker's role as an intermediary between the human and spirit worlds.

Just as shamans merge with their power animal to temporarily construct a new blended energy that incorporates the powers of both beings, transcendent Middle World nature spirits like the Green Man show us that they are literally a part of what they love and protect. It is perhaps this aspect most of all that holds a power for the spirit walker.

Interacting with Transcendent Nature Spirits

Thanks to your offerings, the work done in your square yard, and your gratitude prayers, you are already being recognized by the spirits of the Middle World as one who is choosing to step back into respectful relationship with nature. This makes you very attractive to those spirits who are her caretakers.

The transcendent spirits of Middle World all have their own customs and ways of being. Just as travelers in a foreign country without a good guide may not know when they are making a cultural faux pas until the damage is done, it is important to have assistance in working with these spirits. For this reason, your primary spirit teacher and power animal will be invaluable in helping you know how to interact with these beings and keeping you safe.

That is not to say that these spirits are necessarily ill intentioned, but rather that their world is very different from our own. For instance, they are beings that live beyond our understanding of time and space. A day for them may be a minute, a year, or a lifetime for us. If you went home with them for a day, you might return to find your friends long dead. They might offer you a sumptuous feast that may sicken you or be so impossibly delicious that you would never be satisfied with human food ever again. These examples are to remind you that you need to be thoughtful and have a good guide when interacting with these spirit folk, as the parameters of life are simply different for them.

Exercise: Journeys about Transcendent Nature Spirits

To begin your safe interactions with the transcendent Middle World spirits, it is important to work with your own land or an area close to your home. First, you'll start with a couple of information-gathering journeys.

Take journeys to your power animal or primary teacher (in the Upper or Lower World) to ask:

- "Who are the friendly transcendent nature spirits of this place?"
- "With which of these friendly, transcendent nature spirits may I interact safely?"

Remember to make a gratitude offering to honor your spirit helpers and the natural world after receiving guidance. This helps to strengthen your connections to the world of spiritual power. Give your offerings freely and from heart. Then make notes about what you have experienced in your journey notebook.

Once you have gotten a sense of these spirits, do the following journey to actually meet the spirit your power animal or teacher suggested. As with all Middle World journeys, you will simply leave from where you are in ordinary reality. So if you are journeying in your favorite armchair, ask your power animal to meet you right there and accompany you. In the journey state, stand up and walk outside together—going forward with the instructions below. The questions follow a formula that has been used for many millennia. Following this format upon meeting a new spirit and always remembering to travel with your power animal will help you to reap benefits without falling prey to the pitfalls that can occur when interacting with these kinds of Wild Nature spirits.

Exercise: Journey to Meet a Friendly Transcendent Nature Spirit

Ask your power animal to take you to meet the *friendly, safe* transcendent nature spirit you learned of in your previous journey work. Once you have been brought to the spirit, politely ask these questions in the order in which they are here:

- "What is your name?"
- "What do you want from me?"
- "How can you help me?"
- "How may we work together in harmony?"

Once your questions have been answered, thank the spirit for meeting with you and make a gratitude offering in nature upon your return. Write down the details of your interaction and the answers to your questions. You may also want to sketch this being as you did with those you met in your square yard.

This is an excellent way to begin to get to know a helpful transcendent Middle World spirit. Repeat this entire process until you have met all the spirits who your power animal or teacher feels are safe for you to meet. Remember to use this formula of questions. Each new spirit you meet and get to know better will deepen your connections to the place in which you live.

Your Own Wild Natural Energy

As a spirit walker, you can follow the Green Man's lead and step into your place as one of Earth's shamanic protectors. While often seen as bearded with leaves, a Green Man is sometimes also depicted with leaves pouring from his mouth. We can imagine this as a metaphor for not only embodying our love for the Earth but also speaking or manifesting action on her behalf as well. As we align ourselves with the transcendent Middle World spirits' desires to protect Mother Nature, we can reclaim and remember our own *wildness*.

Andean spiritual teachers refer to our wild energy as *salka*. It is the undomesticated part that lives inside each of us and all other beings of this planet. Domesticated beings are overly rational and materialistic, whereas the wild parts of us live more in our hearts and therefore in harmony with Mother Earth. Through experiencing our wildness and the interconnections interlacing our biosphere, we naturally approach each part of the larger world with a deeper reverence. This allows us to make more respectful choices for ourselves and for the Earth.

Exercise: Awakening Your Wild Nature Energy

Try this breathing exercise to awaken your wild and heart-centered self.

1. With your eyes closed, stand up or sit in an erect posture and focus on your own heartbeat. Listen and feel as it pumps blood through your body. This is your center—where you are tethered to All That Is.

2. Now, stretch your arms out to the sides of your body. Take a sharp breath inward while bringing your fingertips toward your heart. Hold your breath for a heartbeat.

3. Exhale fully and extend your arms again.

4. Repeat step 2. As you inhale, you may see your arms gathering in all of the Earth's love—bringing it to your heart. Allow your energy to mingle with nature's. Inhaling, you are drawing the vitality of the plants, the surge of the tides, the perspective of the soaring hawk into yourself.

5. Repeat step 3. When you exhale and extend your arms again, feel yourself giving energy back to the Earth. As your breath leaves your body, feel the blessings it holds flow over the landscape like the wind—like spring rains caressing a leaf. You are giving the gift of your breath to your green relations, and they in turn breathe it back to the world.

6. Continue in this way for at least ten breaths. *(If you start to feel a little dizzy, take gentler breaths. Please remember to exhale fully so that you don't hyperventilate.)*

7. As you approach your tenth breath remember a time when you felt grateful. If you can, it is especially useful to remember a time when you felt this gratitude during an experience you had in nature. For instance, you can remember the feelings of a cool breeze on a very hot day or how welcome rain feels during a drought. Recall the leap of joy you had at the swoop of a hawk over your car or the sound of coyotes howling on a desert night. Remember your childhood excitement at discovering a storm that had raged while you slept provided a deep enough blanket of white for a snow day! Perhaps you remember an encounter with a deer that watched you without moving. Give yourself permission to recall your own special memory of nature's wonder-filled blessings.

8. Now allow the memory of that time and the feelings of gratitude you had then to fill you up again as you begin to breathe more gently. Allow your breaths to move like ocean waves, grasses wafting slowly in the wind, or the elegant beating of an eagle's wings. Let the gratitude you feel flow out from your heart and extend from your fingertips. With this simple action, you are now radiating healing energies through your body and out into the world.

9. Slowly turn in a circle with your arms outstretched. Allow the energy to keep pouring from your body like an endless, regenerative fountain of light. Imagine this light energy saturating the awakening plants and rising with the sap in the trees. It glitters along the surface of the waters and illuminates the bright plumage of the

returning birds. The newly awakened bear squints as the energy pours over its sleepy head, and the stones—the bones of the Earth Mother—grow ever warmer with your heart's loving touch.

10. When you feel complete with this experience, gently bring your awareness to the place where you are standing or sitting. Smile—if you aren't already—and wiggle your toes and fingers in celebration of your wild aliveness. When you are ready, open your eyes, and look at this world with your newly refreshed wild spirit.

Once you feel able, write down the details of your experience of your wild nature energy. Notice how the feeling may change or deepen your experience of ordinary reality. Ask yourself how you feel about your connection to your helping spirits. Notice how your wild nature energy compares to the energy of the Middle World spirits you have met so far. Leave an offering outside in gratitude for your life.

Listen to your heart to find ways you can make changes that will benefit the Earth and her children. A strong shamanic spiritual practice always includes taking positive action on behalf of the natural world. This can be very simple to start with, but as you practice the above exercise and continue strengthening your wild nature energy, you will naturally feel that you are a part of everything on Earth. From that deep understanding, you will effortlessly develop a stronger desire to be more of a loving force for her nurturance and protection. It is your duty and your calling as one who walks with the spirits.

Figure 21. Altai shaman's drum from Tomsk Province, Russia, late nineteenth to early twentieth century.

Chapter 21

The Middle World as a Source of Power

A **shaman of power** has strong connections to the natural world surrounding the home and strong relationships with the spirits that reside there. Unlike typical people, shamans know all of their spiritual neighbors well and interact with them each day. In turn, the spirits are willing to loan some of their energy to the shamans.

By this time in your journey to become a spirit walker, you have developed strong relationships with your power animal and with teachers in the Upper and Lower Worlds. You have discovered through your journey experiences that these beings provide a spirit walker with clear insights, healing, and spiritual power. As you have followed the exercises in this book, your Middle World sacred place has become a strong center in your spiritual realm. You have also been making regular offerings in nature. All of this preparation has made you ready to enter into relationship with the transcendent and helpful spirits in the Middle World. You have met these spirits, and your connections with them have also begun to grow.

Your strong connections to your power animal(s) and teacher(s) keep you safe from any unbeneficial influences while working in the Middle World. As you now proceed to move more deeply into this realm, always remember to have your power animal and teacher with you. They not only protect you, they will also interpret the information you receive and modulate any energies that may be too much for your physical or emotional body. This will be particularly important later on as you move into working with elemental forces.

~~~~~~

Exercise: Journey to Find Middle World Sources of Power

Here is an excellent introductory question to give you an overview of the potential the Middle World holds for you as a spirit walker. As you have done each time, prepare yourself and your space, and be ready to record the information and make an offering upon your return to ordinary reality.

- Ask your teacher or power animal: "Where are sources of power for me in the Middle World?"

You may be shown specific places, animals, birds, plants, stones, natural forces, or landscape features as a part of this journey. We will be exploring all of these families of beings, and you will be able to find which individuals are willing to be a part of your spiritual community.

You will be starting with animals and birds.

Middle World Aspects of Nature: Animals

Our ancestors had close associations with animals. They used their bodies for food and their hides, bones, and fur to sustain life in other ways. However, among indigenous cultures animals aren't just a resource put on Earth for humans to exploit. Among some cultures, the spirits of animals and birds are considered true kin and are venerated and respected in the same fashion as a person's human ancestors. An animal or bird may even be honored as the origin of the family line. For instance, my stepson is a Haida native from Alaska. He is a member of the Raven clan, and so the raven is honored as his family line's spiritual progenitor.

Across the circumpolar region, there existed bear-honoring rituals.[70] These peoples considered the bear "not only as an animal but mainly as a human being in reverted form, a so-called 'bogatyr' . . ."[71] *Bogatyr* is an Ob-Ugrian tribal word meaning the "son of the Divine Bear Creator." Bears were believed to be responsible for turning the seasons, making berries and fruit ripen, moving the herds, and communicating with all the other "animal peoples." So holy were these creatures that the bear's actual name was never spoken. Bears were referred to by many diverse euphemisms such as The Old One, Owner of the Earth, Old Honey Paws, Old Man/Old Woman of the Moss, Little Mother of Honey, Winter Sleeper, or by using a respectful familial designation such as Grandfather or Grandmother, Elder Brother or Elder Sister, and Uncle or Aunt.[72]

When people in traditional shamanic cultures hunted, fished, and consumed animal and bird flesh, they did so with the utmost respect for their fellow "people" and never took more than was needed. Today it is the role of the shaman to attend to the connections with other beings with whom we share our world. A shaman admires and respects their amazing powers and also seeks to emulate their capabilities. For instance, the shaman may be drawn to work with the strength of a bear, the resourcefulness of a fox, the playfulness of an otter, or the quiet presence of the deer. Some animal spirits become power animals, others are allies, and others may be accessed for their wisdom.

It is particularly useful to become properly acquainted with the animals who share your area. They are an intrinsic part of your bioregion, and their health and well-being are intimately interconnected with your own. Allow this theme of interconnectedness to fuel your explorations. For instance, if the animals that predominate your landscape are prey animals, then learn all that you can about the plants, insects, and other foods they eat and well as the animals that prey upon them. If your area is graced with a healthy, natural predator population, be sure to learn about the prey that they hunt. A shaman always attends to the full circle of existence.

Exercise: Journey to Meet an Animal Spirit near Your Home

In a journey, ask your teacher or power animal to take you to an animal spirit who lives near your home with whom you can begin a relationship. Once you have met the animal, you will ask these questions. Remember to patiently receive the answers to each before you ask the next.

- "How do I honor you?"
- "How can you help me?"
- "How may we work together in harmony?"

Upon your return, remember to make an offering and follow through with any information you received from the animal spirit. Field guides are useful for finding out all the ordinary reality information that you can about the animal. In addition, do whatever you can to help the species in ordinary reality ways by providing water and natural food sources, places to shelter, and by supporting those organizations that work to protect them. Your reward will be a much healthier environment within which to live.

Exercise: Additional Journey Explorations

Take a journey to your teacher or power animal to ask:

- "What animal spirits are most useful for me to work with?" Then, journey with your teacher or power animal, asking them to take you to meet these animal spirits.
- Take other journeys to ask your teacher or power animal to "Please take me to other animal spirits who live near my home."

Continue to connect with all the animal species that live around you. Notice more about how the species are interconnected with each other. Ask them to share information about their connections with you. As you get a deeper sense of your immediate area, begin moving into your larger geographic region by extending your explorations with ever-widening circles. It is also very beneficial to learn the stories that the indigenous people of your region had about the animals. These stories may help you to connect more deeply with those ancient lines of kinship we once universally understood and which you and I are working to refresh.

Middle World Aspects of Nature: Birds

For as long as human memory extends back in time, we have been fascinated by the abilities and appearances of the birds. Their grace and acrobatics fill our hearts with joy, their plumage dazzles our eyes, and their songs delight our ears. While a skilled shaman may fly in journeys through the spirit realms, even the humblest of birds effortlessly sails through the breadth and depth of ordinary reality. As soon as they are able to after being hatched, they take to the air to sail high above the trees and beyond the horizon. Their breathtakingly arduous migrations across continents are miraculous and inspiring. Birds are the unsurpassed natural masters of the Air element.

Here are a few suggestions to help you meet birds that may become part of your spiritual community. The first question is a three-part inquiry that can help you to determine how to enter into and sustain a relationship with a bird spirit.

Exercise: Journey to Meet a Bird Spirit near Your Home

In a journey, ask your teacher or power animal to take you to a bird spirit who lives near your home with whom you can begin a relationship. Upon meeting the bird, you will ask these questions. Remember to patiently receive the answers to each before you ask the next.

- "How do I honor you?"
- "How can you help me?"
- "How may we work together in harmony?"

Upon your return, remember to make an offering and follow through with any information you received from the bird spirit. Look at field guides to find out all the ordinary reality information that you can about your new friend. If your bird friend leaves in winter, learn all you can about the species' migration. Learn how they survive the rigors of migrating thousands of miles. Are there places along the way where you can watch them flock? It is also great to give them the extra support they need to be fully ready for their long flights. Find out what foods are especially good to provide at the end of summer and autumn to assist them with their preparations.[73]

Place your bird feeders near windows to allow for indoor bird-watching. They give opportunities for close-up observation and identification of different species of birds, as well as for studying bird behavior. Along with lots of classic pecking order behaviors, you'll see birds teaching their young to fly and feed, and witness their many calls. You'll also notice that species feed at different times, so over the course of one day, many different kinds of birds can be observed.

Exercise: Additional Journey Exploration

- Journey with a teacher or power animal to ask the bird spirit, "Please give me a *felt* experience of how you perceive the world."

As you did with the animals, continue widening your spiritual community by asking your teacher or power animal to take you to meet other bird spirits.

Middle World Aspects of Nature: Minerals, Stones, and Crystals

While there is much information available these days about the properties of minerals and their relationships to healing and transformation, since you are able to journey, you have the ability to work directly with a stone or crystal rather than relying upon anyone else's explanations. Through journeying, you have the ability to find out a stone or crystal's unique properties as well as to hear its origin story, how it understands the world, how it may become a partner in your practice, as well as how best to care for it.

Even what you may consider a humble pebble has many remarkable stories to tell. Imagine the long journey it has taken. Once a part of a primordial mountain or spewed forth in a molten state by a volcano or part of bedrock laid down as sediment in a primordial sea or crushed by moving continental plates—it has been weathered by rain, pushed along by glaciers, tumbled in oceans, and ground down by billions of thawing and cooling cycles. That little stone has really been around!

Exercise: Journey to Meet a Mineral Spirit near Your Home

As you have for animals and birds, do a journey with a teacher or power animal to a Mineral Kingdom spirit who lives near your home with whom you can begin a relationship. Once you have met the stone or crystal, you will again ask the three introductory questions.

- "How do I honor you?"
- "How can you help me?"
- "How may we work together in harmony?"

Exercise: Additional Journey Explorations

You may also want to journey to ask the stone spirit these questions:

- "Where were you 'born'?"
- "Please give me a *felt* experience of how you perceive the world."

If you are drawn to work with crystals, it is important to determine what it is you want to be doing. Are you drawn to working with minerals for your healing? Are you interested in learning divination? Once you are clear about your purpose, then journey to find out what mineral spirit will be best suited for it. When you know what stone/crystal you are meant to work with, ask these questions of that spirit:

- "How do I choose a member of your family with whom I will work?"
- "How do I clear its spirit body and dedicate it to this work?"
- "How do I dedicate it to my work?"

Once you have procured a stone or crystal in a good way, clear it with the instructions that you have been given. Then ask your power animal or teacher to take you to that specific stone/crystal to ask the three introductory questions again.

Then ask the stone or crystal being:

- "What is the best way to care for you?"

After hearing these answers, you may dedicate the stone or crystal based upon the original information you received from the spirits as well as with any further instructions that you may have received from the actual stone itself.

As you did with the creatures surrounding your home, continue widening your spiritual community by asking your teacher or power animal:

- "Please introduce me to other mineral spirits that are right for me to meet."

Perform your offerings and keep any agreements with the beings with whom you interact.

Middle World Aspects of Nature: Plants and Trees

Plants are the only organisms that can convert light energy from the sun into food through photosynthesis. This is such a remarkable feat that scientists are trying to understand how we can better emulate plants to produce more effective, organic-based photovoltaic cells for a new breed of less expensive solar panels.[74]

Figure 22. Wending through the green. Photo.

As a result of their amazing abilities, plants either directly or indirectly produce *all* of the food that we eat. This includes meat, as the animals we eat either get their own nourishment from plants or nutritionally rely upon prey that itself eats vegetation.

Plants also produce oxygen that is the life-sustaining gas we and other animals rely upon to breathe. The plants take up the carbon dioxide that we exhale and hold it in storage. Indeed, healthy forests are effective carbon storage units. They also provide habitat for animals and birds as well as offer places to find food and raise young. On a small scale, plants provide shade, help moderate the temperature, and protect animals and us from the wind. On a global scale plants in a healthy forest—especially in tropical rain forests—moderate the rainfall patterns over large areas of the planet's surface.

Plants also help to build soil by fixing nutrients from the air. As their bodies die, they release their gathered nutrients into the ground. The resultant organic matter is what works alongside inorganic rock fragments to create healthy soil that sustains further growth. The roots of plants and trees also hold the soil together. A healthy, balanced community of plants and trees reduces erosion. This keeps waterways from becoming choked with silt, slows the progression of pollutants to the oceans, and also keeps hillsides from sliding away.

All life as we know it is intimately connected to the family of plants and trees, so it is time to meet your green family.

Exercise: Journey to Meet a Plant or Tree Spirit near Your Home

Have your teacher or power animal take you to a plant or tree that lives near your home with whom you can begin a relationship. As before, ask the three introductory questions.

- "How do I honor you?"
- "How can you help me?"
- "How may we work together in harmony?"

Follow through with any honoring instructions you received and make offerings to the plant and tree spirits. Along with your usual offering ritual, it is wonderful to sing to the plants. During your singing, you will not only be honoring your connection, you will also be nourishing the plant or tree with your breath. It is best to do this by aligning your back with the tree or if your new friend is a smaller plant, by sitting close to it. Take care not to disturb other plants or the roots and foliage of your new companion.

Exercise: Additional Journey Explorations

In additional journeys, ask the plant or tree spirit for the following:

- "Please give me a *felt* experience of your existence."
- "How do you perceive the seasons?"

- "Please allow me to feel your connection to the Earth."

After each, make sure to take time to make notes and more importantly integrate what you learn. Continue widening your spiritual community by asking your teacher or power animal to take you to meet the spirits of other trees and plants.

Middle World Aspects of Nature: Landscape Features

When I studied with my shaman teachers from indigenous cultures, I found that all of them had developed strong connections to a particular point on the landscape near their home. This place was usually a dominant feature of the area such as a mountain, river, waterfall, glacier, particularly ancient tree, or unusual outcropping of stone. These landscape features worked as focal points for the powers of place and were revered as allies in the shamans' work.

In my own practice, I have become deeply connected to the river that flows near my home. Its many rhythms and aspects are interwoven with my life. In winter, I thank her for not overflowing her banks when the thaw arrives by scattering seeds on her thick ice. This becomes a secondary gift to her birds and little creatures that remain active in the season of snow. As spring arrives, I offer flower petals that rush quickly to the ocean in her tumbling flow. In summer, her quieter stream gets cornmeal which drifts along in swirling patterns amidst busy insects and ripples made by the brown trout, turtles, and frogs. In autumn, when her banks and surface get blanketed in hallucinogenic patterns of color, I sing my thanks to her for another remarkable season and bless her for a good winter.

Developing a relationship with a landscape feature near where you live gives you a deeper feeling of being at home in this world. It magnifies your sense of belonging and roots you to the vibrant spirits of the Earth. Take a look around where you live. What natural features seem most prominent? Open your eyes widely and begin to look for the natural energies that enliven where you reside. It is especially important for those of you who live in cities to do this. The spirits of nature in urbanized areas can use our support. Often, the spirits of nature recede whenever human populations swell an area—especially when the people have forgotten how to be with them. When you enter into relationship with nature and her many spirits, you help to re-inspirit the place where you live. This is a mutually beneficial act as humans feel better and are healthier in places with strong nature spirits.

Exercise: Journey to Meet the Spirit of a Landscape Feature near Your Home

- Journey to meet with the landscape feature you have identified as the most prominent in your area with whom you can begin a relationship and ask the three introductory questions.

As you have done before, follow through with any honoring instructions you received and make offerings to the landscape feature's spirit. In ordinary reality, learn all that you can about your new companion. Begin to get a sense of its part in the larger scheme of your local area. Find out what role it plays in the health of your region. Is it a vital part of the watershed? Does it sustain any at-risk species? Find out all you can about your new "relation." Also learn how you can help to support its health in tangible ways such as cleanups and preservation actions.

Exercise: Additional Journey Explorations

Take additional journeys to ask the landscape feature's spirit for the following:

- "Please give me a *felt* experience of your existence."
- "How do you perceive the seasons?"
- "Please allow me to feel your connection to the rest of the Earth."

Middle World Aspects of Nature: The Forces of Nature

As you will learn in the section on making your shaman prayers through dance, some shamans use dance as a means to affect physical reality. This is logical as nature herself is always dancing to continue creating and recreating our world. All of our physical world—everything that we think of as solid—is in constant motion. On an atomic and subatomic scale, and even on the quantum level, that which makes our reality is always shimmering and vibrating. On a larger level, the elements of Earth, Air, Fire, and Water are in a constant interplay. My primary spirit teacher refers to this as the Dance of the Elementals. We experience these interactions as the forces of nature such as the winds, rain, lightning, thunder, earthquakes, wildfires, volcanoes, erosion, and evaporation.

Inside of us, similar dances continue to recreate our bodies. For instance, your bones are constantly being rebuilt from minerals (Earth Elemental) that were accessed through digestion of food (Earth Elemental). A by-product of this digestion is heat energy (Fire Elemental), which helps to circulate the minerals in our blood (Water Elemental). And all of this is made possible by your constant respiration (Air Elemental), which is also processing hemoglobin (Earth Elemental and Water Elemental), which can transport oxygen (Air Elemental) to your cells to make more energy (Fire Elemental) . . . You get the idea. Neither you, nor I, nor the rest of nature would exist without this elaborate interplay.

The challenge in working with the spirits of the elementals is that they are very different from the other spirits, which may be somewhat anthropomorphized for the sake of easy communication. The elementals are simple, faceless, raw power. Since that is the case, you may wonder how you can step into *reverent participatory relationship* with an elemental. I find that learning to interact with the forces that they produce is a far easier way to begin as they are more familiar to us.

Since you have already learned about the great, spherical wheel of the directions, you can use that framework to begin interacting with the winds. As you may already know, certain wind directions signal different weather patterns and carry different scents or qualities. For instance, where I live, an east wind carries the salty scent of the ocean, while a southerly wind brings warmth and moisture.

The high- and low-pressure systems that are a part of weather patterns stir the winds in different directions. A high-pressure system which usually brings fair weather turns in a clockwise direction. Here in Maine, a high-pressure system carries dry, cooler air down from Canada and often means we'll be seeing more brilliant blue skies. Low-pressure systems usually carry storms and precipitation and pull a heavy quilt of clouds across the sky.

Before you begin this work, do your ceremony of honoring the directions. This is a way to remember that the wind in each direction may carry some of the energies of its quadrant in the sphere of creation. Also practice your grounding exercise as these forces can be quite powerful and working with them can sometimes leave you feeling a little off balance.

Before the journeys to each wind indicated below, it is also a great idea to stand outside and face the direction for a few moments. Give yourself full permission to align with each direction before your journeys. Notice your feelings, scents, and other sensations without judgment. When you feel aligned, do the following journey work.

Exercise: Journeys to Meet the Spirit of the Winds

Journey to a teacher or power animal and ask it to take you to meet with the spirit of each of the winds. Don't try to do these all in one day! Each wind carries the energy of one of the elementals more strongly and will be best suited to support your work with that elemental. Take time to meet and get acquainted with each wind and in so doing begin to get acquainted with the elemental forces.

Have your teacher or power animal introduce you. Once you have been introduced to the spirit of the each wind, ask the spirit the following questions.

- "How may I work with you safely?"
- "How do I honor you?"
- "How can you help me?"
- "How may we work together in harmony?"

After you have gotten your answer, thank the spirit of the wind you met and return to ordinary reality. After you have made notes and grounded yourself, go out and do an offering of gratitude. Follow up with anything that you received from the spirit of the wind.

Developing a connection with the winds can support you to have a better spiritual understanding of the weather. Since the winds are an active dance between the fire of the Sun and the Air, we can begin to step into harmony with both of those spirits as well when we work with the winds.

Process Questions

- How does your experience of the weather differ from the way that you felt about it before you met the four winds?
- Think about how a better understanding of the winds and their connection to weather could benefit your daily life.

A New Sense of Home

Now that you have met each different neighbor around your residence, you can have a richer experience of the place where you live. Indeed, this sense can continue to radiate outward so that you develop the deep feeling of being truly home in a way that very few people experience. This is a shaman's view of ordinary reality. That is, that the world around you is alive with beings, they are connected directly to you, and all these spirits are a part of the Whole that also embraces you. As a spirit walker, you are never alone. As you strengthen your relationships with the other beings in your world, you will find that you are more comfortable in other aspects of your life as well. When you enter into a relationship with the beings that surround you, a sense of confidence grows inside you that supports more ease in your human interactions. I call this experience one of being more comfortable inside of your own skin.

To strengthen your sense of home even further, it is now useful to see all the aspects you have met in Middle World actually working together. The intricacy of the Dance of Life is quite breathtaking. Being able to glimpse even a small slice of that marvel is one of the gifts of a spirit walker.

Exercise: Journey to Experience a Deeper Sense of Your Home

Journey with a teacher or power animal to experience the intricate web of interconnections around your home by asking:

- "Please give me a *felt* experience of how all the spirits that I've met in the Middle World around where I live are connected."

  Record your impressions and all that you experience in this journey.

Process Questions

- Articulate, as best as you can, in your journal the bodily, emotional, and spiritual sensations of getting to know the "neighbors" around your home and their elaborate interconnections. Remember to make an offering outdoors to thank the spirits whose dance together makes your home.

Chapter 22

Shaman Prayers—Dancing and Movement

In Western culture, it is very easy for even the most dynamic spiritual practice to become an intellectual exercise. To prevent this, it is important to include your body in your practice. Just as nothing in nature is ever static, it is essential for the shaman, as a part of nature, to move. While you may not think of yourself as a dancer, it is important to incorporate movement into your spirit walker practice. From a spiritual perspective, adding a physical component to your practice supports you to be fully embodied and therefore much more powerful. Walking in nature is an excellent way to exercise your body and be more in the world with wonderful chances to glimpse your new bird and animal friends. It can be a great idea to get specific direction from your trusted power animal or teacher about movements that can strengthen not only your body but also your connections to the spirit world.

For our ancient ancestors, there was no need to go to the gym. They lived lives in which they were in constant motion. Walking, running, lifting, carrying, and other constant tasks kept them more fit than many gym-goers in our contemporary culture. Work was a part of life that was not separated from being joyful—it couldn't have been since so much of a person's existence was dedicated to the physical activities of survival. For this reason, a work routine was often accompanied by singing to make the efforts more pleasurable. This way of being is still practiced in rustic agricultural or herding societies. Songs are used to instill work with liveliness for the purpose of lightening the labor. Groups engaged in repetitive activities such as planting, harvesting, and hauling water might also use song to help coordinate the team members' efforts. Difficult tasks would then become a series of rhythmic, patterned movements. Once you are moving in rhythm, it is a very short leap to dance.

Most of us danced when we were children. We spun in circles, jumped for joy, and skipped as easily as breathing. Perhaps it is time again to connect movement with a joyful spiritual practice instead of something we have to do. Even if we are limited in our ability to move, we can dance. Your movements can be small and slow, and forms of dancing may even be done without moving the legs or feet. After all, trees dance in that way every time the wind blows.

Our movements can be a form of prayer and may be used to alter the physical reality around us. The biologist Lyall Watson wrote in 1976 about his magical encounters with an Indonesian shaman woman who, by performing a ritual dance, was able to make an entire grove of trees vanish into thin air.[75] In other chapters of his account, Watson chronicles how dance is used for many purposes including healing, honoring of the spirits of nature, and for shamanic initiation ceremonies. Indeed, so much of the magic worked by shamans on this island was created through movement and dance that Watson referred to this place as the "Island of the Dancing Shamans."

Exercise: Dancing Journey

- Journey to a teacher or power animal to ask, "How can my dancing alter my world?"

As you get a sense of the power your dancing can have on yourself and your surroundings, it is important to find out how you can use this inherent power to support the health of the world around you.

- Ask your teacher or power animal to "Please give me a dance that is healing for the land."

When you come back from this journey, practice the dance for ten to thirty minutes until your body has the movements memorized. When you feel you've got it, make notes about the journey and do your offerings.

- In a separate journey to a teacher or power animal, ask, "What is the best way to use this dance (when, where, etc.)?"

Once you are clear about how you can use this dance, begin to practice what the spirits have given you. If the dance is meant to be done on the new moon or at the turn of the seasons or even weekly—mark your calendar so that you do not forget to pray with your body.

Journey Explorations

Take journeys to your teacher or power animal to ask for this information:

- "Please give me a movement that is healing for my body."
- "What is the best way to use this movement? When and where should I do it?"
- "How does my moving my body assist in the healing of All That Is?"

When you return from these journeys, practice the movements your received and record any additional information you have received. After each interaction, make an offering of gratitude.

Process Questions

- Articulate, as best as you can, in your journal the bodily, emotional, and spiritual sensations of learning to move for a spiritual purpose.
- How has your perception shifted about movement and dancing?
- What movements have the most power for you?

Chapter 23

Shaman Prayers—Storytelling

From a shamanic perspective, stories have incredible power. They can paint the picture of an era, give you courage, keep history alive, help to prepare you for a life event, teach you about a skill, and so much more. You can learn how to take your intentional use of language and heal, soothe, and enfold a child or support a person to leave the world as they are dying.

I am a fortunate woman, as my entire childhood was filled with stories. I was the firstborn and entered the world at a time when many of my elders were still living. Not only did I have two sets of grandparents, but their siblings were also a part of my life. I was blessed to spend many hours with my great grandmother, who had several living siblings, as well. More importantly, all of these elders were storytellers. No matter how difficult their existence may have been, their stories held a vibrancy and were generally well seasoned with humor and laughter.

For orally based tribal cultures, storytelling was a way to preserve the accumulated wisdom of history and transmit all that to succeeding generations. Stories included the tales which explained the cosmos, mythic stories of their ancestors, how their people came to be, how to hunt with respect, proper behavior, and much more. Imagine an encyclopedia of knowledge shared one story at a time! Children in an oral culture would absorb the collective wisdom through the elders' tales in a way that wasn't very different from my own childhood.

When the written word became paramount, oral traditions began to die out. This is unfortunate, as it contributes to the unraveling of traditional cultures. As ethnic and tribal groups lose their stories, they lose the glue that holds them together, and what was once an intact culture starts to die. When people no longer have cultural supports, they lose an important rudder for finding a way through the world. Then, as cultures die, people themselves can become lost, falling into spiritual illness, depression, anxiety, drug addiction, and alcoholism.

Learning stories and how to share them is a part of a shaman's journey. While there are very few spiritual storytellers who are living, there are legions of them in the spirit world. Storytellers of every tradition and time period are available to those who can walk between the worlds. Working with your primary teacher and your power animal, here are some journeys to begin learning about the power of stories.

Exercise: Journey to Meet a Storytelling Teacher

Journey to your teacher or power animal to have them take you to a storytelling teacher. Ask that teacher:

- "What is your name?"
- "How do I honor you?"
- "How can you help me?"

Journey Explorations

Once you have a better sense of how you can respectfully work together, these are some other rich story questions you may want to take into journeys:

- "How did this world begin?"
- "What are the stories the spirits share about me?"
- "What is the story I am meant to tell to the world?"
- "How do I let go of the parts of my old story that hold me back?"
- "What is the story I need to be telling about my life now?"

Chapter 24

Traditional Shamanic Healing

*I*n its most elemental form, shamanic healing attends to the spirit of a person, animal, or place. It does this by removing spiritual energy that doesn't belong and filling the being up with spiritual energy that is necessary, beneficial, and harmonious. This unburdens the body and mind of the patient so that health and balance are returned. While being guided by her or his power animal and teacher, a shamanic practitioner can release an intrusion. The resulting void is then filled with beneficial energy by a teacher or power animal—effectively replenishing the patient's divine light.

The ceremony to release unbeneficial energies is called *extraction*. When a person exhibits signs of having intrusive energy in her or his body, these intrusions may be first noticed as a feeling of being internally "off balance." A massage therapist or polarity or energy worker may observe "blocks" in the person's energy system. An acupuncturist may feel impediments to the circulation of life force, while a traditional osteopath may perceive a foreign essence overlaying the person's original matrix. These clues may be indicating that an intrusion of unbeneficial energy exists. If you experience these kinds of indications in your body, your helping spirits can remove the spiritual intrusions.

Common Causes of Intrusions

You may be wondering how such energies get into someone's body in the first place. There are several common causes that contribute to intrusions.

Intrusions as a Result of Soul Loss

You and I are designed to be completely filled with the divine light of our spirits. Indeed, we are spirits that chose to embody so that we could experience and affect the physical plane. While here, we are affected by the other beings with whom we interact and the circumstances in which we grow. During our lives, we may experience situations that diminish our light. Indeed, life situations may cause you to lose portions of your essential energy. These can include past or present physical or emotional traumas, surgeries, accidents, or a loss. When your essential soul energy becomes lost, free-floating energy from the environment may enter your body to fill the void. Since this energy is not your own, it becomes an intrusion.

Intrusions Created by Emotional Discharges

Intrusive energy forms can be produced when many human beings in an area generate feelings of intense fear or anger. Such powerful discharges of negative emotional energy often occur as a result of a battle, terrorist attack, a calamity such as a bridge or tunnel collapse, the sinking of a large oceangoing vessel, or even a natural catastrophe such as a severe earthquake or hurricane. The resulting energy from many people expressing terror or rage produces a lingering miasma over the area that can enter the spirit bodies of those living in proximity to or visiting the site. This form of intrusive spirit illness can occur even decades after the precipitating event unless the energies that were produced are cleared. If lives have been lost during the precipitating event, these sorts of intrusive energetic pools may also be haunted by numerous restless spirits who can cause spiritual illness in those who enter the area.

There are certain instances whereby an intrusion is placed inside a person by another person. In cases of extreme rage or jealousy, a person may unconsciously throw off huge amounts of what we Westerners describe as negative energy. These are destructive thought forms which, when created, may take on their own life as a very primitive sort of entity. Most people experience how the very air in a room is changed by an angry person's outbursts. If this anger is directed at someone, the person in question may be intruded upon by that thought form entity. The same is true of jealousy. If you are the focus of that jealous energy, you may become the victim of an intrusion.

Intrusions Produced by an Illness/Parasite

There are some physical conditions that can produce their own intrusive energy. When the disease is perceived as taking over the patient—that is, an illness has a life force that seeks to dominate or destroy its host—it may be just such an intrusion. For instance, if a patient is suffering from an infestation by a parasitic organism, the energy of the parasite as well as its physical form is sharing the patient's body.

Intentional Intrusions

These kinds of intrusions occur when someone is intentionally cursed or a person's rage has been directed toward them. The former is more common in some traditional societies and/or immigrant communities where unbeneficial forms of magic or witchcraft are practiced. In such situations, the person who is choosing to harm another places spells or curses upon member of the community with the intent to cause trouble.

Another case is common in every human community. A person shaking a fist or finger in fury at another person produces in them a series of small energetic "darts" which may enter the focus of their anger as intrusions.

Illness Transference

In these circumstances, the person chooses to take on another's spirit illness either consciously or unconsciously. This is most often seen among those patients who are unable to hold personal boundaries in relationship with other people. They may live through or for another person, attempt to control other people, blame others for their problems, have a sense of being a victim, or attempt to fix other people by sacrificing themselves on behalf of another. This behavior is more common in people raised in dysfunctional families and in the partners and children of alcoholics or addicts. The blurring of personal boundaries produces a situation whereby intrusive energies can be easily passed from one person to another. This may sometimes be a multigenerational issue where entire families share similar spiritual illness or "family curse."

Do You Have an Intrusion?

You are fortunate in that as a spirit walker, you have the key to connect with the unseen world and have powerful companions to assist you in your endeavors. Your power animal and teacher are also able to help you through their caring and healing. If you resonated with the discussion of intrusions, you may want to journey to your helper spirits to see if you need a healing extraction.

～～～～～～～～～～～～～～～～～～～～～～～～～～～～～～

Exercise: Journey to Receive a Healing from Your Teacher or Power Animal

- Journey to your teacher and/or power animal to ask, "Do I have unbeneficial spiritual energy in my body?"

If your spirits answer in the affirmative, don't be afraid, but simply set aside time as soon as you can to allow them to work on your body. Once you have prepared your space and yourself, enter into a journey to your teacher and/or power animal to ask them to give you a healing.

A shamanic healing usually includes their scanning your spirit body for the intrusive energy, removing the energy, filling you with beneficial, harmonious, and healing energy, and then sealing your spirit body. When they are through, it is important to thank them and then to do an offering of gratitude for their loving care of your spirit.

Allow some time to pass and notice what you feel. At a later time, you may want to ask your power animal or teacher to explain how you can spiritually protect yourself and attend to keeping your spirit whole.

It is important for your health and well-being to keep yourself filled with your own spirit and to keep that spirit fully enlivened. When you are truly full, there simply isn't any room for intrusive energy! Like eating well and exercising support the strength of the physical body, attending to the health of your spirit keeps you free from spiritual illnesses. If you feel that you require more healing than this journey provides, contact a shamanic healer near your home.[76]

Process Questions

- If you required a healing, articulate, as best as you can, in your journal what is was like to discover that you had an intrusion.
- Write down what the experience of being healed was for you.
- When you feel ready, journey to ask your power animal or teacher how you can better keep your spirit body fully enlivened.

Chapter 25

Renewing Your Soul's Light

Keeping yourself fully enlivened is the very best way to keep your spirit whole and well. For this reason, it is important to renew your soul's light on a regular basis, especially after an emotional shock, a loss, a time of trouble, or after having had an extraction.

Singing, dancing, and praying in the many different ways you have learned in these pages are some ways to keep your spirit light burning brightly. The following exercise is another powerful way of keeping yourself more fully spiritually vibrant. It is a way to invigorate the soul—renewing the light of your spirit.

Exercise: Renewing Your Soul's Light Meditation

This process begins very much like the Embodied Light meditation practice you have already learned. Once you've read the meditation, find a quiet time and space where you will not be disturbed and listen to the guided version at *www.myspiritwalk.com* through headphones.

As with all other shamanic work, create a sacred container by honoring the directions and perhaps lighting a candle or burning some of your favorite incense. Relax your body into a comfortable position by sitting yourself down in a chair that allows your back to be straight with your feet on the floor.

1. With your hands folded gently in your lap, close your eyes and take a few moments to breathe. Allow your breaths to be both quiet and full—somewhat like the breaths of the deep sleep state.

2. As you begin to more fully relax, notice that your breath originates in the center of your chest. Imagine a light there that grows brighter with every breath you take.

3. As this light grows brighter, see it also expanding to fill your entire body—growing ever brighter.

4. Allow your light to expand so that your physical body is enfolded in light. Your spirit—your light—completely surrounds your body. This is your true state of being.

5. While continuing to breathe, notice how your radiant body is connected to the radiant body of the Earth. Your body moves within the atmosphere of our planet. You live by swimming through her air with your feet touching her body. Your body is held by your light and is always cradled by the Earth.

6. Allow yourself to reach out even further and feel how the Sun's radiance embraces the Earth as she embraces you in her loving warmth. Allow all your senses to be fully enlivened by this nurturance.

7. You are a divine and magnificent aspect of All That Is. Light is what connects you to All That Is.

8. Invite your beloved power animal to join you and reveal its radiance to you. If any thoughts or feelings arise that limit your light, invite your power animal to help you to release them gently. These limitations fall away effortlessly like leaves blowing in the wind. As this happens, your light blazes brighter!

9. Now in your full illumination, allow yourself to play together with your radiant power animal. Dance together as two sacred beings of light.

10. As you and your power animal are completely luminous, you now are able to perceive that all of nature around you is light, too. You are a part of the limitless fabric that unites All That Is.

11. As you continue your breathing, allow the limitless, eternal radiance that is all around you to add even more brilliance to your body of light. Every bit of your being is luminous, beautiful, and dazzling!

12. Your soul is pure, exquisite light—strong, healthy, and renewed to its magnificence.

13. In this state of renewal, allow gratitude to fill your heart. Let yourself fill to overflowing. As you become replete with gratefulness, it naturally pours forth from your body in all directions. Like a glorious fountain, light enters you from All That Is, and gratitude pours a luminous nourishment back to All That Is. You are being filled and pouring forth simultaneously—in a beautiful circle of energy. When you feel complete with this, give thanks to your power animal and allow yourself to gently move your body.

14. Breathe deeply and begin to slowly return your attention to the room in which you are sitting.

15. Gently bring your full awareness back to ordinary reality. You hold the feelings of your light and gratitude as you take another full, deep, sighing breath.

16. When you feel ready, gently open your eyes—renewed, refreshed, radiant.

When you feel ready, you may wish to make notes about what you experienced while doing this meditation. Take time to record all that you felt, saw, and heard. If you feel ungrounded after this meditation, go outdoors and do your grounding exercise. Make an offering to give thanks to all the plants, trees, animals, and birds—radiant beings all!

Process Questions

- Articulate, as best as you can, in your journal the experience of having your soul's light renewed.

- How do your current feelings differ from the way that you felt before you did the exercise?

- Think about how you could include this practice regularly in your life. Record your impressions.

Chapter 26

More Healing Experiences

Through initiatory experiences like the ones in our journey exercises, the spirit walker can more firmly hold on to the knowledge of being part of the fabric of All That Is. These experiences produce new memories that can help the spirit walker defy the illusions of the senses and establish feelings of connection that become unshakable.

Indeed, one of the greatest challenges we face as human beings is to sustain our deeper ways of knowing ourselves and the world while being fully immersed in our ordinary life. Sometimes, the illusion of separateness creeps back into our consciousness or we fall prey to the limiting beliefs that we may still carry. At these times, it is most important to focus upon your gratitude practice and repeat the Renewing Your Soul's Light meditation. You are not only transforming yourself as you do this; you are also participating in the transformation of what we currently understand as being human.

If old beliefs or old feelings continue to diminish your spirit, take the concerns to your trusted power animal and teacher. Ask them to help you unravel the old entanglements in your psyche that interfere with you being able to know yourself as a beautiful, sacred being. Remember, these unbeneficial thoughts and feelings are usually just incorrect perceptions that you learned in your early life. Because our senses are limited, human beings make incorrect assumptions about who we are and the nature of the world. We then pass these misperceptions on to subsequent generations—both consciously and unconsciously.

You and I are fortunate to be living in a time when many more people are willing to release those outmoded perceptions. More and more, people like you are clearing away any thoughts and feelings that are incongruent with their divine light. This allows *all of us* to become more conscious cocreators of this reality. As a spirit walker, you also have access to effective ritual journeys to assist you in this work.

Dismemberment as a Healing and Initiatory Experience

Very early in this book, I mentioned that traditional shamans often have one or more experiences of initiatory death and rebirth as a part of their training.

These experiences usually involve a stripping away of the initiates' ordinary way of perceiving reality and a partial loss or detachment from the personality or ego self. These ecstatic experiences include some form of dismemberment or dissolution of the physical body. This spiritual annihilation of the old self is a ritual way for initiates to "die" and then be reborn as a shaman.

In the ritual, initiates have some sense of being partially or totally obliterated. While in the shamanic state of consciousness, they might be partially or completely eaten by animals or demons or burned up in a fire or torn asunder by the forces of wind and ice or ground to dust. The shamanic initiates would allow the apparent destruction of their physical body by the spirits in order to be free from the old life as an ordinary person. While the physical body is dismembered, initiates would be experiencing true consciousness—true spirit—as a witness to the destruction. This would allow a visceral sense of the power of spirit and its ability to move beyond the body. Indeed, this loss of the old body would

Figure 23. Dismemberment-Rememberment (detail) As an initiate releases outmoded, unbeneficial perceptions of self during a dismemberment ritual, she or he can be "reborn" as a spirit walker. My primary teacher gave this curious figure an outer envelope of skin with my face. My spirit was then allowed to flow into the doppelgänger-like replacement body that was literally made from aspects of All That Is. Pen and ink drawing, 20 x 30 inches.

More Healing Experiences   199 support initiates to attain a kind of shamanic enlightenment. That is, initiates would be freed to perceive the radiance of spirit that unites all things and beings.

Once the old body is destroyed and the spirit is revealed, the second phase of the ritual begins. That which is unmade through dismemberment is subsequently remade by the compassionate spirits. During this part of the experience, there is a renewal of the initiates' flesh; however, this new body is often made differently or has different components than the original.

For instance, while still in the shamanic state of consciousness, initiates might see that their bones have been replaced by crystals, that their new heart is now the heart of an animal, or that all internal organs are now light or stones. In my own dismemberment, I was remade by a legion of helping spirits, each of whom brought a gift of a plant, shell, crystal, star, or animal and placed it on a table. The objects, which came from every region of the Earth and from the heavens above, were piled into the form of a human body.

While all this may sound horrifying or at the very least somewhat daunting, the dismemberment journey has the purpose of healing.

Embarking on a Dismemberment Journey

In a tribal society, the dismemberment experience was a deep initiation with an added effect of healing the initiate. In many cases, the person called to be a shaman would experience an unexplained physical malady or a kind of madness which did not respond to common methods of healing because it was actually a spiritual sickness. After the dismemberment ordeal, this illness would finally be cured.

As a contemporary spirit walker, you can utilize a dismemberment journey as a path to fully opening up to the power you carry in this lifetime. The reason that this can be such a powerful form of healing is that very few people are actually able to perceive their wholeness and marvelous abilities. The result is that very few ever live to their fullest potential. Through the dismemberment, you can ask that anything that is unbeneficial to you—anything that spiritually interferes with you being able to live your fullness—be altered, dissolved, or released.

In our culture, the negative aspect of the egotistic self—what defends and glorifies our separateness—is what most needs to be dismembered or dissolved away. The egotistic self is what continually fuels the "us and them" mentality, reinforces our feelings of being powerless, and so drives human beings to seek power from others. It creates an unhealthy autonomy and obscures or seeks to destroy our divine self.

When we deeply know our connection, feel our oneness with the Universe, and unshakably understand the existence of our eternal soul-self, we have transcended the limitations of our personality's egotistic nature. We can then have a healthy sense of self that allows us to function in the world and which understands our connection to the Whole. We can discern what is safe or not in our environment without projection, organize our lives, synthesize information, and be creative. Dismemberment is a tool to release the dark grip of the ego so that the light of our divine self may shine through.

The dismemberment exercise is best done over a longer period, and you will want to prepare ahead of time so that you will not be interrupted. I recommend that you set aside a full day for this work. You will be doing a full sixty-minute journey to allow you a rich experience and require at least a couple of hours of quiet time and grounding afterward. For this purpose, it is best to have a full-length shamanic journey drumming CD. There are several good ones available on the market.[77]

Choose a day that allows you to be outdoors in a safe place during the time after the journey. Your new spirit body will grow stronger as you sit quietly with the spirits of nature and allow the shifts you have experienced to settle. After about an hour or so of being outside, eat lightly and then do your grounding exercise. It is also important to make an offering of gratitude to the spirits for their gift of healing. After that, you may wish to journal your experience. As you are able, do all of the post-journey work outdoors. Initially, you may feel your senses are heightened. In my personal experience, the natural world seems a great deal brighter, more vibrant, and more beautiful after this experience.

Remember, that even if the dismemberment seems frightening, it is a healing from your most trusted spirits. As much as you are able, surrender to their care so that you can receive the most benefit. The dismemberment journey is a pathway to lose egotistic interference and be one with the Universe. It is also an experience that will support you to be much more strongly present and grounded in your daily life on this glorious Earth. When you know yourself as a divine, eternal being, you no longer long for the world beyond this one. You recognize that even the most mundane experiences are part of the beauty that makes us all. It also helps you to realize that whatever is happening in your life, it is just one small part of your existence. That wider perspective makes your mortal life ever sweeter and can heighten your love for the Earth.

Exercise: Dismemberment Journey

Journey to your most trusted teacher or power animal to ask it to:

- "Please dismember me so I am freed from unbeneficial perceptions that limit my life journey."

When you return, follow the instructions I have outlined, and take plenty of time outdoors to support you to regain feelings of being grounded and present. Notice how the world around you now smells, looks, and sounds. Also take time to observe how you feel, what you sense, and what thoughts come to mind. All of these are a part of the experience. If at any time you feel too uncomfortable, ask your power animal to help you and also keep practicing your grounding exercise. Make gratitude offerings; eat and drink water to help you be fully present in the physical world. These actions will allow you to get comfortable in your new body.

Process Questions

- Articulate, as best as you can, in your journal the bodily, emotional, and spiritual sensations of being dismembered.
- How do your feelings differ from the way that you felt before you experienced it?

Record all that you notice.

Chapter 27

More Explorations of Time

Time is both multidimensional and dynamic, with all moments existing in a simultaneous *now*. As a result, your past lives and future lives have a direct impact on your current life experience. In other words, although the pervasive illusion of human *consensus reality* has convinced us that time is linear, you are actually in other time streams while you are in this one. Realizing this opens up a way of looking at your history, your past lives, and possibilities for the future in an entirely fresh way. Waiting for you in another parallel band of time are gifts and understanding that another part of you already holds. This is all accessible to you since, as a spirit walker, you are able to step outside of ordinary reality. Through your journeys it is possible to have experiences outside of your current time period or location in space.

This capacity is quite marvelous for several reasons. First, it allows you to go outside of current time to a point in the past to rework an experience for healing. Imagine being able to bring your power animal or teacher with you to a frightening childhood experience. You can also visit and speak with those who have died to reconcile an old hurt, learn a skill your relative never had a chance to teach you, or visit a place or structure that is no longer standing. The possibilities are endless.

Past Life Journeying

One of the most exciting things about stepping outside of time is to experience your multidimensional self. Since all time is happening now, you are also experiencing all your lifetimes simultaneously. You can visit another version of yourself to learn a skill or gain a perspective you need in this time-space frame. For instance, if you are shy about singing, ask your teacher to take you to meet with a self in another lifetime who can share a love of singing with you. Your spirit teacher could arrange a meeting with an aspect of your multidimensional soul that is able to speak with the plants or animals to become even more connected to nature in this life. Another interesting experience would be to meet with a past self who was a shaman, healer, or oracle. Let your brilliant imagination guide you in the direction of your explorations and always have your power animal and teacher with you to support the work.

Exercise: Journey to Meet a "Past Self"

- Journey to your teacher and/or power animal to ask, "Please help me meet a past self who can share a skill that I need now."

Trust your teacher or power animal to guide you. Once you have learned the skill, give thanks to your past self for his or her generosity and return with your teacher to your current time frame. As always, make a gratitude offering in nature to thank your spirits and to honor your multidimensional self.

This journey can be repeated many times to help you get a deeper sense of the breadth and depth of your soul experience across time. I find that this kind of journey helps to give the lifetime I am currently experiencing a richer context.

Past Life Journeys for Healing

Many people today speak about wounds or traumas they had in a past life to explain something being amiss in this current life experience. While knowledge of such things is useful, it is far better to be able to work with spirit to heal whatever is causing the impediment to your being able to live fully and freely. Through the work of your loving teacher and power animal, many past life experiences can be resolved to the point where the trauma or injury no longer impacts your present lifetime.

Exercise: Journey to Heal a Past Life Issue

- Journey to your teacher and/or power animal to request, "Please help me to resolve an issue in a past life that needs to be healed."

As before, allow the teacher or power animal to guide you to the appropriate experience and do the healing on your behalf. When you return from your journey, make an offering. While you are outside, pick up a small stone to represent your healed self. Carry this stone in your pocket or in your medicine bag[78] to help you remember the power of the experience.

Back to the Future

What we think of as the future is not fixed or predetermined. Since time has fluidity and depth, there are many possible futures laid out ahead of us. The future is created in the present through the feelings we radiate into the world, the thoughts we have, and the actions we take now. Through journeying, you can take voyages into possible futures to help you to make good decisions about the situations that present themselves in your current experience. I'm not talking about metaphorically skipping to the back of the book to see how things turn out, but rather I am suggesting that working *consciously* in the present with some foreknowledge of possible outcomes can support you to make wise choices in your life. These conscious choices continue to weave your future from moment to moment. With the ability to journey and check your progress, you can work in concert with your teachers to create a future that is most beneficial.

Process Questions

- Write down, as best as you can, what it was like to work with a part of yourself in a different time period.

- How does this experience change your perception about time?

- How do you believe accessing other versions of yourself can support your life now? Record your thoughts and impressions.

Chapter 28

Shaman Prayers: The Journey of Transcendence

We are wired to transcend our historical experience of being human. Because of our remarkable biology, the power of our feelings, and the eternal nature of our spirits, we are designed to evolve into fully conscious, loving creator beings. At this time, there is an ever-growing group of people who are engaged in this transformation. Since we are connected through the nonlocal field, we can energetically support one another's spiritual evolution. Through disciplined practice we can effect transformations in every aspect of our life, and these internal changes make big changes in the world around us. As Sandra Ingerman and her association of teachers repeatedly show in the Medicine for the Earth[79] work, we are capable of producing concrete, measurable miracles, such as healing polluted water, simply through the action of transforming ourselves.

Exercise: You Are the Light of All That Is Meditation

This practice is an expansion of the Renewing Your Soul's Light meditation that produces a healing effect in yourself and throughout your world. It is an opportunity to step into your fullness as a sacred human being who is both divinely physical and divinely radiant! As you become more unshakable in the full awareness of your extraordinary nature, you transcend old definitions of yourself and move closer to becoming a new, more powerful human being. Before you listen to the mp3 audio file found at *www.myspiritwalk.com*, "You Are the Light of All That Is," prepare yourself by reading the meditation through a few times.

1. While comfortably seated, close your eyes and take a few moments to breathe. Allow your breaths to be both quiet and full—somewhat like the breaths of the deep sleep state.

2. As you begin to more fully relax, notice that your breath originates in the center of your chest. Imagine a light there that grows brighter with every breath you take.

3. As this light grows brighter, see it also expanding to fill your entire body—growing ever brighter.

4. Allow your light to expand so that your physical body is completely filled with light.

5. While continuing to breathe, notice how your radiant body is connected to the radiant body of the Earth. Your body is held by your light and is always cradled by the Earth.

6. Allow yourself to reach out even further and feel how the Sun's radiance embraces the Earth as she embraces you in her loving warmth. Allow all your senses to be fully enlivened by this nurturance.

7. You are a divine and magnificent aspect of All That Is. You and everything else are radiant.

8. Invite your beloved power animal to join you and reveal its radiance to you. If any thoughts or feelings arise that limit your light, invite your power animal to help you to release them gently. These limitations fall away effortlessly like leaves blowing in the wind. As this happens, your light blazes brighter so that you are completely transformed into pure light!

9. Now in your full illumination, allow yourself to play together with your radiant power animal. Dance together as two sacred beings of light.

10. Every bit of your being is luminous, beautiful, and dazzling!

11. Allow your power animal to help you to perceive the center of the light of All That Is—the radiant source of All. You are a sacred part of Creation—no more or less important than any other part. Let yourself fully experience that your life is an aspect of that radiance dancing on the Earth. Your beautiful body is pure, crystallized radiance!

12. Your radiance is a healing force, and your Earthly body is a sacred temple infused with that light—shining on all the beings around you. Your soul's pure, exquisite light renews your body and renews the world around you to its magnificence. Allow yourself to feel harmony. Feel peace. Fill with the love for All That Is.

13. Let yourself fill to overflowing. As you become replete with harmony, peace, and love, more light naturally pours forth from your body in all directions. Like a glorious fountain, endless light enters you from All That Is. At the same time, your radiance pours a luminous nourishment back to all beings. You are being filled and pouring forth simultaneously—in a beautiful circle of energy.

14. When you feel complete with this, give thanks to your power animal and allow yourself to gently move your body.

15. Breathe deeply and begin to slowly return your attention to the room in which you are sitting.

16. Gently bring your full awareness back to ordinary reality. You hold the feelings of your light and gratitude as you take another full, deep, sighing breath.

17. When you feel ready, gently open your eyes—renewed, refreshed, radiant.

Practice this state of being as often as possible to renew not only your own body, but also to transform the environment around you, helping to bring balance and harmony to the life-forms, the soil, the water, and the air of our beautiful planet.

Process Questions

- Articulate, as best as you can, in your journal the experience of being pure light.
- How do your feelings differ now from the way you felt before you practiced this?

Chapter 29

Sustaining Your Practice as a Spirit Walker

The best way to keep your spiritual path vibrant is by thinking of your life as a playground of transformation. In other words, while you will have the normal ups and downs all human beings experience, you have support available to move through them with a great deal more grace than most. If you have followed the steps presented thus far, you have been given the tools to prepare you for whatever comes. What we'll discuss here are steps to help you when you stumble, lose your passion for this way of being, or just have times of feeling stuck.

Cultivating Compassionate Curiosity

As you have been working diligently with the material of the previous chapters, you will have been transforming not only yourself, but also contributing to transforming our shared reality. This process, like all things in nature, involves a constant, evolutionary persistence to keep the heart of who you desire to be fresh and enlivened. To better move through the times when you don't feel as connected to your path, it is important to cultivate a willingness to stretch into places that seem beyond your comfort zone and lovingly investigate yourself—to observe your thoughts and your actions. Each of us has many aspects of self—an inner wise person, the inner child or children, an inner critic, and so forth.

We also have a part that can observe our multifaceted self with compassion. If you feel unsure about this aspect of your psyche, try the following journey.

Exercise: Journey to Meet Your Compassionate Observer Self

- Journey to your power animal or teacher and ask to meet "My observer self who is compassionately curious."

Once you meet that part of yourself, develop a relationship with this aspect as you have done with the other spirits you have met over the course of your spirit walker path. This part of your inner self can be an essential ally when something disturbs the rhythm of your practice.

In life, we often we run up against inner interference that temporarily throws us off course. When we wear the eyes of our compassionate inner detective, we can recognize that these interferences are actually calling our attention to some perception, thought, or feeling that needs to shift. You are creating your world through your perceptions and their resultant thoughts/actions. Therefore, your willingness to be more conscious through self-observation is a key to changing not only yourself, but *through you*, the outer world as well. Remember, as a cocreator, your adaptations automatically begin to change everything.

Remember that the following steps are not linear. Even though all of them are essential, you will need to go back and forth through them in different ways at different times.

Eliminating Inner Interference

Many of the inner stumbling blocks we encounter in our lives are subconscious perceptions, outmoded beliefs, and entrenched habits. In order to understand them, it is useful to begin to look at what energies motivate your behaviors. At the core, human behaviors spring from love or fear.

The motivation of love produces:

gratitude, compassion, appreciation, caring, wonder, mercy, sympathy, harmony, admiration, thankfulness, empathy, benevolence, exhalation, patience, tenderness, courage, thoughtful regard, and . . . more love.

Fear expresses itself as:

anxiety, anger, jealousy, envy, doubt, judgment, blame, shame, depression/shutting down, bitterness, holding yourself back, feelings of being a "victim" or "inferior," power abuse, impatience, emptiness, cowardice, suspicion, and . . . more fear.

In the larger culture, people use many methods to avoid feeling their fears, one of which is even projecting their fears onto others. These methods prevent a person from identifying their fears so that they can be cleared away.

Unbeneficial coping mechanisms include:

procrastination, distraction by keeping busy, staying involved in other people's dramas; holding on to emotional pain to avoid moving forward; blaming others, intimidating others, identifying others as enemies to externalize the fear; excessive use of alcohol, narcotics, food, sex, TV watching, or computer games; hoarding to shut feelings down.

Since your subconscious mind can be such a strong source for your actions and thoughts, it is useful to begin observing yourself so that you can get a clearer sense of what is happening below the surface of your mind.

This means being willing to engage your compassionate inner detective to observe how you are in the different aspects of your life. Most of us behave very differently in different situations. Take the time to notice how you are at work and at home. Notice how you behave in relationships. Begin observing how you think, what language you use about yourself and others, and those times when you are judgmental. Also look at how you deal with disappointment and notice what is happening inside yourself when you forget to be engaged in your shamanic practice.

Exercise: Compassionate Observation

Once you have observed yourself in a *compassionate* manner, it is time to ask yourself the following kinds of questions through journaling or journeying. Again, be gentle with yourself as you are doing a kind of inner work that will eventually free you from the unbeneficial patterns and beliefs that interfere with your life and your spiritual practice.

- "Why did I think that?"
- "Why did I react that way?"
- "What are the patterns I consistently fall into?"
- "What do they reveal about where I am in my process?"

Continue to pay attention to what you learn and see how you can begin to become more conscious about your thoughts and actions. As you pay attention to your thoughts and actions, you may begin to notice that many of your difficult moments involve strong feelings. Conscious and unconscious perceptions held in your mind blend with the input of your emotional body and exit as feelings. Sometimes, the feelings you express have little or no connection to what is actually happening in the present moment; instead, they are often connected to past events and the perceptions you developed then.

Many of our interference patterns are actually connected to our anxiety or fears—even unconscious ones that are difficult to recognize. With the assistance of your compassionate and curious inner detective, you can look at the ways your fears reveal themselves in your behavior. Often, human beings use certain responses to circumvent or try to diminish anxiety. Our fears and anxieties usually trigger the fight/flight/freeze response as mentioned in chapter 4, The Creative Power of Emotions. While it is easy to recognize a literal fear response, we may not readily notice a fear when it is cloaked in a behavior.

For example, if you become controlling, blaming, argumentative, or bossy in certain situations, that is a form of the fight reaction. On the other hand, if you become vague, withdrawn, confused, or emotionally immobile, you can think about it as a freeze reaction. If in response to a situation you easily lose patience, give up, or repeatedly don't have enough time to do something, then you may be expressing a form of flight. Compassionately notice these aspects of your behavior—they are very human. Catching these behaviors is the first step of disabling the fear behind them. The prize is to relinquish the grip your unconscious fears have on your life.

As you continue compassionately observing yourself, make notes about when feelings come up and under what circumstances. Developing a picture of your reactions will support you in digging a little deeper. An excellent method is to journey to a teacher or power animal to ask questions such as "What fear is underneath this behavior?" As you bring your fears into the light of consciousness, you loosen their grip on you. Fears brought to the surface can be healed far more easily than ones that are hidden in the depths of the unconscious mind.

As your fear becomes clearer, see if it has a message for you. Remember, the original, initial emotion was trying to give you information about your environment. By finding out more about the fear, you can begin shifting out of your old, dysfunctional behavior and learn new ways of being that are healthy and can contribute to moving you forward.

Exercise: What Does Your Fear Reveal?

You may find it useful to ask this question of your teacher or power animal in a shamanic journey: "What is my fear trying to reveal to me in support of my spiritual evolution?"

Once you discover your fears, you need to follow through and heal them. Remember, powerful spirit walkers do not hide behind excuses. They clear away any interferences to spirit so that power and harmonious energy can flow in a natural and beneficial manner.

Using Gratitude to Make You More Resilient

Making changes in your life can be stressful, but gratitude has a healing effect on the body. People who choose to practice gratitude regularly are able to sustain their positive biochemistry and regulate their moods even when stressed. In other words, the continued practice of gratitude allows individuals to have a physical and emotional resilience that was not accessible before.

Exercise: Creating a Shamanic Gratitude Journal

Start with a beautiful notebook.

1. Begin the gratitude list on the first right-hand page with the following sentence: "I am grateful for the cocreator,_____." Put your *own* full name on the line.

2. On a new right-hand page, start with the line: "I am grateful for these beings who made my life possible: _____." On that blank line, place the names of your parents and grandparents. This is important to do *even* if they were not nurturing presences. Their only gift may have been to give you life, but what a wondrous gift it is!

3. Then add on the same page, "I am grateful for these people who nurtured me to wholeness: _____." On this part of the list, add the names of every teacher, friend, therapist, relative, coworker, or neighbor that gentled your path.

4. Continue using only right-hand pages as you add new sections to your list.

5. Now start a list of all the role models living and dead who have inspired you with this sentence: "I am grateful for these people who helped me to know my life could have meaning: _____." This is the place to list historical people and others whom you may have never met and yet have positively impacted your life. Add all of your heroes, heroines, and inspirations to the list.

6. Start a fresh page to be grateful for your body with this heading: "I am grateful for these aspects of my physical body and its marvelous abilities." List all of your senses, the abilities you have to move your body, and your ability to feel.

7. On the next page add, "I am grateful for these other beings who shared my life." This is the place to list all your animal and bird friends. List all of your pets and then include any amazing animal and bird sightings you have had over your life. Remember all your encounters—the deer who stood and watched you, the hummingbird that hovered nearby, the butterfly that landed on your shoulder, a turkey vulture rocking in the sky, the chattering chipmunk that made you giggle, the formation of geese you heard at dusk. Whatever beautiful animal and bird memories you have, put them on the list.

8. Broaden your list to include the following on the next page: "I am grateful for these places and the experiences I have had in them." Write down everything you can think of that you are grateful for in nature on the list. Include all the stunning sunrises and sunsets you've been fortunate to experience. The times you went into nature and felt beauty, majesty, and awe. Include rainbows, full moon nights, fireflies on a summer evening, the aroma of the pine, sea smoke dancing over the ocean, a fresh snowfall—reach deep into your memory and pour it all down on the pages.

Feeling gratitude helps you to nurture the seeds of your new spirit walking self. As each of us commits to being grateful, it becomes possible to bring the dream of a peaceful and loving world to fruition.

All over the world, millions of people are practicing the art of becoming grateful, conscious cocreators. My partner and I are seeing a growing commitment to this path among both our shamanic healing clients and the folks we work with in our training programs. Each of them gains a more visceral sense of the radiant connections that unite all of our cosmos and also begins to perceive the impact each of us has upon that whole. This personal experience in turn awakens the desire to only create *positive* ripples through the web of life. These people commit to this in spite of personal struggles, fears, illness, or other disruptions because they realize it is the best hope for our world. They also realize that becoming a grateful cocreative force makes it much easier to be peaceful and loving even in difficult times.

When my partner and I presented at the 2001 International Conference of Science and Consciousness, we also had the opportunity to attend to a lecture by Peter Russell, a fellow of the Institute of Noetic Sciences and author of several books including *The Global Brain Awakens, The Consciousness Revolution,* and *From Science to God.* In his lecture, he shared that any shift occurring in the square root of 1 percent of a population is able to produce a meta paradigm shift throughout the entire population. Globally, that means that a critical mass of a little more than 8,360 people[80] living their lives in a heart-centered, harmonious way—every day—can literally change the planet. For this to happen, we need to be willing to get out of the old ways of unconsciously reacting and learn healthy ways of consciously responding to our world.

Expanding Possibilities—Shamanic Imagination

Hopefully, through the explorations you have made with the help of this book you already recognize that the shamanic journey process—like all methods which expand humans beyond their ordinary ways of perceiving the world—is an extraordinary tool for moving beyond your mind's limitations. Being able to *feel* experiences and new possibilities before they are physically realized allows your mind to cooperate more readily. Use the journey process to stretch into new places of consciousness and shift out of old beliefs that limit you. Expanding your perceptions of what is possible actually helps you to realize new ways of being and grow beyond your circumscribed comfort zone.

In addition, the unconditional love and guidance that the transcendent spirits offer can buoy you up and give you courage to keep going forward. Their expressions of compassion can support you to have more compassion for yourself.

Getting Support from the Human World

We human beings are social primates. There is a reason that solitary confinement is considered a harsh punishment. In the psychological theory referred to as Maslow's hierarchy of needs,[81] the primary human need is for physiological support—such as food, water, and shelter—followed by the need for safety and the need for social relationships. When people don't have the close connections of family, friends, and larger social groupings, they are much more susceptible to loneliness, social anxiety, and clinical depression.

Especially during those times when you are engaged in making changes in your life, it is important to become an active participant in supportive communities. This may mean that you need to be willing to stretch into places that feel uncomfortable by meeting new people, going to gatherings, and taking classes. Supportive, social relationships can help you to integrate all that you are learning and experiencing as your shamanic life continues to unfold.

On the other hand, you may also find that you have to let go of older relationships that do not support your growth. This is usually something that occurs organically. In the course of our evolving, some of our human connections occasionally grow apart.

While it can often be emotionally difficult to experience this kind of change, it is also true that as one person leaves you, you become open for others to enter into your life.

If at any point you need even more support than your friends and family network can provide, give yourself full permission to seek out a professional, such as a therapist or counselor, especially skilled at assisting people along their life paths. Good counselors are worth their weight in gold in helping to sort out feelings or untangle patterns that are too overwhelming to deal with on your own.

Being Compassionately Persistent

There is no substitute for being willing to pick yourself up when you falter or stumble on your path. Indeed, our journeys through life are seldom straight. They are usually a long series of starts, stops, twists, turns, and restarts. So long as you give yourself permission to look at all of your life as exuberant explorations on your playground of transformation, you can keep making progress with no limits upon how far you can go.

When you falter, stall, or get lost along the way, remember to repeat all the steps in this chapter. At those times when I feel that nothing is happening or that my spiritual practice seems less valid, the phrase "Absence of evidence isn't necessarily an evidence of absence" gives me the courage to just continue moving forward.

Keep journeying to let go of expectations around timing and to get support around any disappointments that may arise along your path. Remember to keep integrating all that you learn in your journeys and through the rituals and exercises in this book, too.

Process Questions

- Write down in your journal what it was like to meet your inner observer. How does it feel to have him or her support your process?
- What did your fears reveal to you about your subconscious beliefs?
- Articulate, as best as you can, in your journal the bodily, emotional, and spiritual sensations you received while learning about your fear.
- How are your spirit teacher, power animal, and spirits in the Middle World helping you work with this fear?
- Are you able to go back to the practice of gratitude when you stumble or feel stuck?
- Are you journeying regularly to keep getting spiritual support?
- Are you willing to reach out for more support from a counselor to work with your fears, so that you can become an even more powerful person?

Record all that you are feeling and thinking about this.

Chapter 30

Genuine Power

By the time you've made it this far, you have gathered quite a bit of information about yourself and the way shamans approach life. While all of this is important to developing a deep shamanic practice, just learning all the skills, mastering techniques, and finding out how to perform rituals don't make anyone a powerful spirit walker.

Genuine power comes from the ability to live one's life in an exceptional way. This is certainly true of the masterful tribal shamans with whom I have studied and many of the Western masters who have imparted their wisdom to me. Each of them shared a common trait of being scrupulous about keeping their minds, hearts, and actions in harmony and in coherence with spirit.

The path of this way of life includes much of what I have already shared in these pages. Let's look now at a clear breakdown of the elements that are necessary to make this a reality.

Being Precise with Spirit

It is essential as a spirit walker that you work tirelessly to keep your communications with Spirit perfectly clear. It is not enough to be somewhat certain about Spirit's messages. A powerful spirit walker is disciplined about maintaining clear communications and keeping ego out of the way.

Being Impeccable in Your Relationships

Keeping good, honest relationships with *all* beings is the hallmark of a true and powerful spirit walker. Indeed, *reverent participatory relationship* is the standard in which all interactions are engaged whether they are with the beings of nature such as animals and birds, the spirits, or other humans. All relationships, intimate or casual, at work or at home, or with complete strangers should be engaged in in a heartfelt, authentic, and fully present manner.

"Walking Your Talk" without Exception

The phrase *walking your talk* refers to being constant and earnest about keeping actions in complete harmony with your words. While many people say one thing and then do another, this is not the behavior of a person of power. Truly, your actions do speak louder than your words, and when these actions flow from the harmony of an aligned heart, mind, and body, they have a significant impact upon the people and other beings around you. As a spirit walker, your words are always truthful, and they are always backed up by appropriate action—holding yourself fully accountable for your thoughts and behaviors.

Living in Gratitude

I have said much about gratitude in these pages, but it cannot be stressed enough that gratitude can function as a foundational core which brings about a harmony both within and around you. Indeed, gratitude resonates in and around the body with a vibration very similar to that of love. It is healing, harmonizing, and capable of shifting humans out of their negative thought and feeling patterns, often in miraculous ways. As such, it is necessary to practice this loving and grateful state in all aspects of your life: in your spiritual practice, at home, at work, in friendships, and with strangers you meet.

Living Life as a Sacred Ceremony

Loving-kindness, patience, and true caring flow effortlessly from a grateful heart. This makes it easier to eliminate the perceptual separations between the sacred and profane aspects of your life. Those times when you are doing the laundry, washing dishes, walking the dog, or commuting to work are all opportunities to erase the limiting boundaries that cause you undue emotional discomfort. If all work is sacred work, then even the most arduous or tedious task can be done with a peaceful heart and even with bursts of joy!

When I was still commuting, I would often be stuck in traffic for an hour or two. Instead of fussing about how terrible my situation was, I learned to look around for animals, birds, and other aspects of nature while I was stopped. It got to be a kind of game. More often than not, I was treated to a soaring hawk, a deer browsing at the edge of the woods, a flock of geese, or some other beautiful sight even in the most urban of settings. These events cheered me greatly and made the difficult task lighter. When I shared my sightings at work, I also realized that many of my coworkers who traveled the same traffic-choked roads rarely saw what I was blessed to see. Later on as my shamanic practice evolved, I realized that by changing my way of perceiving my commute, I was able to experience what others in the same situation could not. This understanding has stayed with me as a great example of how a shift in attitude changes everything.

No Excuses

Powerful spirit walkers take full responsibility for their behavior. They are careful and considered about all interactions. This means not "copping out" by blaming the situation, your past, or another person for what you are doing or for what you say. Your continued, steadfast application of the methods you have learned to center, ground, and relieve negative emotional states keep you in coherence. As a spirit walker, you understand that you are the master of your life and you are cocreating your reality with every feeling, thought, word, and deed. As a result, you work at keeping coherence between your heart, mind, and body so that your thoughts, feelings, and actions are always in complete, conscious alignment.

Releasing Ego

Powerful spirit walkers diligently work on whatever feelings or perceptions inside hamper them from being able to be in the world in a good way. That means tracking down the machinations of the meddlesome ego, uncovering unconscious, limiting beliefs, or changing the perceptions that create inner dissonance.

Like the Greek god Janus, destructive ego has two faces. The first is the superior attitude that one is somehow fundamentally better than someone else or some situation being experienced. This face of ego represents the braggart and boaster. The actions of this destructive side of the ego try to make others feel insignificant. They also cause a person to behave in pretentious and sometimes reprehensible ways.

The reverse face of destructive ego is the one that expresses deeply seated beliefs of inherent unworthiness, insignificance, or inferiority. It tells you that you are unable to attain a state of grace, to be good enough, that you are less than other people. Both expressions of ego are symptoms of *separation*. The "I" becomes more important than the truth that you are always part of a larger and more splendid "we." No person, no being, no thing can be separate from the divine. It is inherently impossible!

The spirit walker tames this inner tyrant through the practice of gratitude, of engaging with helpful healing spirits and other people on a similar path, and through cultivating the deep recognition that no part of All That Is can be any more or less important than any other.

"Do or Do Not. There Is No Try."

The character Yoda from the Star Wars series offers us this simple truth. Being a spirit walker isn't about trying to do anything. Instead, you choose to bring feelings and thoughts into alignment and then take action. One heartfelt choice and its subsequent action, followed by another and another, are a spirit walker's lifework. If you don't immediately succeed at a goal or purpose, you continue to make the choice to realign and take action. As a result, you incrementally move forward. Since all is sacred, the path toward the goal is equal to the goal itself. Each is of equal merit and deserves full focus and attention in collaboration with Spirit.

Process Questions

- Articulate, as best as you can, in your journal the bodily, emotional, and spiritual sensations of shifting your focus to the process rather than the goal.

- How does the way you are living now differ from the way that you felt before you began working with the material in this book?

Conclusion

Sacred Living as a New Paradigm

As shamanic practitioners—spirit walkers—we want to make sure that future generations have a healthy world in which to flourish and grow. This book is meant as a support for you as one of those wonder-full people. It is my goal to inspire your heart, nurture your hope, give you courage, and engage your mind with both magical and practical solutions for your life.

It is my heart's desire that all you have read in these pages will help you to be in alignment in your thoughts and actions, to be in heart coherence with the spirits that are around you, and to dissolve divisions between what you consider to be sacred and mundane. It is time that all aspects of life are woven together as sacred work.

This isn't always easy, as it demands that we become mindful and heart-centered in all of our actions. To become more fully conscious, each of us needs to confront those times we fall asleep in our lives, choose to shut down, go into our heads, or function on autopilot. From a place of consciousness, we can behave in a more reverent way and choose to fully and lovingly participate in our lives and in all our relationships.

I believe that we are in a complex dance of relationship with a multitude of beings in every moment. The spirits of nature, animals, plants, and other humans with whom we share the planet are truly "all our relations."

In the sixteenth century, when the Native American nations of the Haudenosaunee gathered into what is referred to as the Iroquois Confederacy, one of their tenets included that in every deliberation, we must consider the impact of our decisions on the next seven generations.

As enough of us learn to live in *reverent participatory relationship* with the spirits, the Earth, and all of her creatures, this relationship will become the dominant way of being for *all* people. As that day is dawning, we embrace our world—pulling it back from the brink so we can deliver it safely into the loving care of all future generations of human beings. It is my profound wish for you that, in your travels along the path of the spirit walker, you get to participate in these remarkable, positive changes.

In Gratitude

Grateful blessings to the fabric of light which embraces
and continually creates all matter.

Blessings to the boundless cosmic ocean in which our
planet rides.

Blessings to this beautiful Earth of whom we are a part
and on whom we depend.

Blessings to the spirits of all directions, above and below.

Blessings to all the magnificent creatures with whom we
share this world.

Blessings to the loving ancestors who passed us the torch
of life.

Blessings to these amazing physical bodies for embodying
our spirits.

Blessings to our senses with which we can explore and
savor our lives.

Blessings to those we hold close and those heart connections we cherish.

Grateful blessings to all beings—may we shine our lights
brightly all our days.

With hearts full of gratitude, we honor that we are all
one.

BLESSINGS TO YOU ON YOUR PATH,
EVELYN C. RYSDYK

Resources

Organizations

Circle of the Sacred Earth: *http://circleofthesacredearth.org*
Foundation for Shamanic Studies: *www.shamanism.org*
My Spirit Walk (source of support material for this course): *www.myspiritwalk.com*
Nepalese Shamanism for Peace and Brotherhood (Bhola Banstola and Mimi Genitrini): *http://www.nepalese.it/en*
Shaman Links: *www.shamanlinks.net*
Shamanic Teachers and Practitioners: *www.shamanicteachers.com*
Shaman Portal: *www.shamanportal.org*
The Society for Shamanic Practitioners: *www.shamansociety.org*
Spirit Passages (author's website): *www.spiritpassages.com*
True North Health Center (The author offers shamanic healing in this integrative medical center in Falmouth, Maine.): *www.truenorthhealthcenter.org*

Periodicals

The Journal of Shamanic Practice: The Society for Shamanic Practitioners: *www.shamansociety.org*
Sacred Hoop Magazine: *www.sacredhoop.org*

Other Sites of Interest

Chapel of the Sacred Mirrors (Art of Alex Grey): *www.cosm.org*
Institute of HeartMath: *www.heartmath.com*

Video Links

An interview with Bhola Banstola titled "Interview Bhola Nath Banstola" can be found on *youtube.com*.

Many other shamanic videos may be found at: *www.shamanportal.org*
under Shamanic Videos

Bibliography

The American Heritage Dictionary. Boston: Houghton Mifflin Co., 1985.

Avila, Elena, RN, MSN. *Woman Who Glows In The Dark*. New York: Jeremy P. Tarcher/Putnam, 1999.

Bower, Bruce. "Raising trust." *Science News* 158/1 (July 2000).

Braden, Gregg. *The Isaiah Effect: Decoding the Lost Science of Prayer and Prophecy*. New York: Three Rivers Press, 2001.

Calderon, Eduardo, Richard Cowan, Douglas Sharon, and F. Kaye Sharon. *Eduardo el Curandero: The Words of a Peruvian Healer*. Richmond, CA: North Atlantic Books, 1982.

Castaneda, Carlos. *The Teachings of Don Juan: A Yaqui Way of Knowledge*. New York: Washington Square Press, 1968.

Comings, Mark, PhD. *The New Physics of Space, Time and Light*. From his keynote speech given at the 2005 True North Annual Conference, Portland, ME: 2005.

Czaplicka, M. A. *Aboriginal Siberia, A Study in Social Anthropology*. London: Oxford University Press, 1969 reprint of the original 1914 edition.

Devlet, Ekaterina. "*Rock art and the material culture of Siberian and Central Asian shamanism*." In *The Archaeology of Shamanism* edited by Neil Price, 45. London and New York: Routledge/Taylor & Francis Group, 2001.

Eliade, Mircea. *Shamanism: Archaic Techniques of Ecstasy*. Princeton, NJ: Princeton University Press, 1964.

Greene, Brian, PhD. From an interview with Brian Greene discussing his new book, *The Hidden Reality: Parallel Universes and the Deep Law of the Cosmos* with Terry Gross on the WHYY program *Fresh Air* which was aired on National Public Radio on January 24, 2011.

Greenpeace. "Human Impact of Man-made Chemicals." London: Greenpeace, 2003; *www.greenpeace.org.uk*. Accessed January 28, 2011.

Grey, Alex. *Transfigurations*. Rochester, VT: Inner Traditions International, 2001.

Halifax, Joan. *Shaman: The Wounded Healer*. London: Thames Hudson, 1992.

———. *Shamanic Voices: A Survey of Visionary Narratives*. New York: E. P. Dutton, 1979.

Harner, Michael, PhD. Interview reprinted in *Shaman's Drum Magazine*, Number 71.

———. *The Way of the Shaman*. New York: HarperCollins Publishers, 1990 edition.

Harner, Sandra, PhD. "Shamanism and the Immune Response," The Frontiers of Consciousness Lecture Series. Institute of Noetic Science; San Francisco: June 26, 2002. From a CD recording of the lecture produced by The Foundation For Shamanic Studies, Mill Valley, CA, 2002.

Harner, Sandra, PhD, and Warren W. Tryon. "Psychological and Immunological Responses to Shamanic Journeying with Drumming." *SHAMAN* 4/Nos. 1–2 (1996).

Hawkins, David R., MD, PhD. *Power vs. Force: The Hidden Determinants of Human Behavior*. Carlsbad, CA: Hay House, 1995 (2002 edition).

Holmes, Hannah. *Suburban Safari: A Year On The Lawn*. London and New York: Bloomsbury Publishing, 2005 (US edition).

Ingerman, Sandra. *Medicine for the Earth*. New York: Three Rivers Press, 2000.

Institute of HeartMath. *Science of the Heart: Exploring the Role of the Heart in Human Performance,* a bound overview of research conducted by the Institute. Their website is: *www.heartmath.org*; access to their research is available on this site.

Intimate Strangers: Unseen Life on Earth, Tree of Life. Episode originally broadcast on public television 1999. A & E Home Video, 1999.

Joralemon, Donald, and Douglas Sharon. *Sorcery and Shamanism.* Salt
Lake City: University of Utah Press, 1993.

Kelly, Karen. "Thorbjorg's Story, An Introduction to Seiðr." *Spirit Talk,*
Early Summer 1999, Issue #9. Spirit Talk is an online core-shaman-
ic newsletter available at: *www.shamaniccircles.org/spirit_talk.*

Louis, Roberta. "Shamanic Healing Practices of the Ulchi." *Shaman's
Drum Magazine* 53 (Fall 1999).

Mack, John E. *Passport to the Cosmos.* New York: Crown Publishers/
Random House, 1999.

Masterson, Kathleen. "From Grunting To Gabbing: Why Humans Can
Talk." *All Things Considered,* National Public Radio, aired on
August 11, 2010. A transcript may be found at: *www.npr.org/tem-
plates/story/story.php?storyId=129083762&sc=emaf.*

McClenon, James, PhD. "The Experiential Foundations of Shamanic
Healing." *Journal of Medicine and Philosophy* 18 (1993): 107–27.

Monterey Bay Aquarium. *"Animal Guide."* Monterey, CA: *www.mon-
tereybayaquarium.org/animals/default.aspx?c=ln,* accessed January
20, 2010.

Nagishin, Dmitri. *Folktales of the Amur: Stories from the Russian Far
East.* New York: Harry N. Abrams, Inc., 1980.

Narby, Jeremy, PhD. *The Cosmic Serpent.* New York: Penguin/Putnam,
1998.

National Science Foundation. "Scientists Offer New View of Photosynthesis." Press Release 07-052, May 7, 2007. *www.nsf.gov/news/
news_summ.jsp?cntn_id=108534,* accessed May 18, 2007.

National Wildlife Federation. "Garden for Wildlife: Backyard Habitat
Certification Information." *www.nwf.org/Get-Outside/Outdoor-
Activities/Garden-for-Wildlife/Certify-Your-Wildlife-Garden.
aspx?campaignid=,* accessed May 8, 2011.

Pearce, Joseph Chilton. *The Biology of Transcendence: A Blueprint of
Human Spirit.* Rochester, VT: Park Street Press/Inner Traditions
International, 2002.

Petrovic, Boris. "Overtone-Singing/Throat-Singing." *www.docstoc.com/
docs/21849609/Overtone-Singing-Throat-Singing,* accessed Sep-
tember 30, 2010.

Pringle, Heather. "New Women of the Ice Age." *Discover Magazine* 19/4 (April 1998).

Rysdyk, Evelyn C. *Modern Shamanic Living*. York, ME: Samuel Weiser, Inc., 1999.

———. *A Spirit Walker's Guide to Shamanic Implements*. Yarmouth, ME: Spirit Passages, 2012.

Schwartz, Gary, PhD, and Linda G. S. Russek, PhD. *The Living Energy Universe*. Charlottesville, VA: Hampton Roads Publishing Company, 1999.

Talbot, Michael. *The Holographic Universe*. New York: HarperCollins Publishers, 1992.

Tolkien, J.R.R. *The Lord of the Rings*. New York: Houghton Mifflin edition, 1984, originally published in 1954.

United States Fish and Wildlife Service, "Where the River Meets the Sound, An Educators Guide to the Nisqually National Wildlife Refuge." Third Printing, 2004; *www.fws.gov/nisqually/pdf/Educator_Guide.pdf*.

Vitebsky, Piers, PhD. *The Shaman*. Boston, New York: Little Brown and Company, 1995.

Wardwell, Allen. *Tangible Visions*. New York: Monacelli Press, 1996.

Watson, Lyall. *Gifts of Unknown Things, A True Story of Nature, Healing and Initiation from Indonesia's "Dancing Island."* Rochester, VT: Destiny Books, 1991; originally published, New York: Simon and Schuster, 1976.

WGBH/PBS, "Parallel Universes," episode of the series *Nova*. Boston: WGBH, 2011.

Winkelman, Michael. *Shamans, Priests and Witches: A Cross-Cultural Study of Magico-Religious Practitioners*. Tempe, AZ: Arizona State University Anthropological Research Papers, No. 44, 1992.

World Health Organization. "The World Health Report 2003" – *Shaping the Future*. Geneva, Switzerland: 2003 (World Health Organization website: *www.who.int/phe/en*).

World Wildlife Fund Canada. "Reducing Your Risks To Pesticides." WWF, Toronto, Canada: 1998. An Internet version is available through WWF, UK: *www.wwf.org.uk/filelibrary/pdf/risk.pdf*.

Notes

1. Quote from my spirit teacher, Grandma Henderer, who is also my great, great grandmother.
2. *Intimate Strangers: Unseen Life on Earth, Tree of Life*, originally broadcast on public television 1999 (A & E Home Video, 1999).
3. Jeremy Narby, PhD, *The Cosmic Serpent* (New York: Penguin/Putnam, 1998), 125–31.
4. John E. Mack, *Passport to the Cosmos* (New York: Crown Publishers/Random House, 1999), 83.
5. Gary Schwartz, PhD, and Linda G. S. Russek, PhD, *The Living Energy Universe* (Charlottesville, VA: Hampton Roads Publishing Company, 1999), 53–73.
6. Mircea Eliade, *Shamanism: Archaic Techniques of Ecstasy* (Princeton, NJ: Princeton University Press, 1964), 33–66.
7. This was my personal experience during a prolonged journey in which I was dismembered.
8. Michael Harner, *The Way of the Shaman* (New York: HarperCollins Publishers, 1990 edition), 22.
9. Ibid., xi–xv (preface to the third edition).
10. James McClenon, PhD, "The Experiential Foundations of Shamanic Healing," *Journal of Medicine and Philosophy* 18(1993): 107–27.
11. Eliade, *Shamanism: Archaic Techniques of Ecstasy*, 100.
12. Ibid., 23–24.
13. Piers Vitebsky, PhD, *The Shaman* (Boston, New York; Little Brown and Company, 1995), 22–25.

14. Michael Harner, PhD, in an interview reprinted in *Shamans Drum Magazine*, Number 71, pp. 16 & 24.

15. From the April 2005 presentation for the Academic Departments of the Glasgow Homeopathic Hospital, "Creating Therapeutic Encounter."

16. Vitebsky, *The Shaman*, 99–100.

17. Mark Comings, "The New Physics of Space, Time and Light," from his keynote speech given at the 2005 True North Annual Conference.

18. Ibid.

19. Hewlett Packard UV Absorbtion Spectrophotometer.

20. At the 2001 Conference of Science and Consciousness, author Gregg Braden stated that the U.S. military advanced this test by separating the samples by fifty miles.

21. Much of the scientific research in this section may be found in *Science of the Heart: Exploring the Role of the Heart in Human Performance*, a bound overview of research conducted by the Institute of HeartMath. Their website is *www.heartmath.org* and access to copies of their research is available here.

22. David R. Hawkins, MD, PhD, *Power vs. Force: The Hidden Determinants of Human Behavior* (Carlsbad, CA: Hay House, 1995; 2002 edition), 128.

23. His teachings may be found at *www.gratefulness.org*.

24. Hawkins, *Power vs. Force: The Hidden Determinants of Human Behavior*, 128.

25. For instance, while some traditions may use tobacco as an offering, the preponderance of waste tobacco in our environment has caused harm to our amphibian friends such as frogs and salamanders.

26. Instruction for such a pouch may be found in the *Spirit Walking Tools & Implements* e-book on the website *www.myspiritwalk.com*.

27. Vitebsky, *The Shaman*, 14.

28. Evelyn C. Rysdyk, *Modern Shamanic Living* (York, ME: Samuel Weiser, Inc., 1999), 29.

29. *The American Heritage Dictionary* (Boston: Houghton Mifflin Co., 1985), 1179.

30. This is being reinforced by the work of the Foundation for Shamanic Studies MONOR (Mapping of Nonordinary Reality) project. For many years, this organization has been collecting maps of shamans' spirit worlds. In examining and comparing these maps, incredible similarities are being discovered.

31. Vitebsky, *The Shaman*, 14.

32. Harner, *The Way of the Shaman*, 53.

33. A quote from Grandma, my primary spirit teacher.

34. Carlos Castaneda, *The Teachings of Don Juan: A Yaqui Way of Knowledge* (New York: Washington Square Press, 1968), 11.

35. Ekaterina Devlet, "Rock art and the material culture of Siberian and Central Asian shamanism," in *The Archaeology of Shamanism* edited by Neil Price (London and New York; Routledge/Taylor & Francis Group, 2001), 45.

36. Ker Than, "New Type of Ancient Human Found—Descendants Live Today?" *National Geographic Daily News, http://news. nationalgeographic.com*, accessed December 22, 2010.

37. Lyall Watson, *Gifts of Unknown Things, A True Story of Nature, Healing and Initiation from Indonesia's "Dancing Island"* (Rochester, VT; Destiny Books, 1991; originally published in New York by Simon and Schuster in 1976).

38. *Science News*, "Quantum Theory Demonstrated: Observation Affects Reality." *www.sciencedaily.com*, accessed January 2, 2009.

39. Michael Talbot, *The Holographic Universe* (New York: HarperCollins Publishers, 1992), 139.

40. Vilmos Dioszegi and Mihaly Hoppal, ed., *Shamanism in Siberia* (Budapest, Hungary: Akademiai Kiado, 1996), 91.

41. *www.nwf.org*

42. The National Audubon Society is a wonderful resource for field identification information. Their website *www.audubon.org* can help you to locate your local Audubon chapter.

43. If your square yard is indeed in a suburban yard, I recommend that you read the book *Suburban Safari: A Year On The Lawn*, by Hannah Holmes. In this book, you will find out how one woman, armed with her insatiable curiosity and a notebook, discovers all the rich and varied life in and around her yard. It's a delightful read!

44. The book, *A Spirit Walker's Guide to Shamanic Implements,* is available at: *www.myspiritwalk.com.*
45. *Dictionary.com. Collins English Dictionary - Complete & Unabridged,* 10th edition. HarperCollins Publishers. *http://dictionary.reference.com/browse/ceremony,* accessed August 24, 2010.
46. While this sounds like a long procedure, it isn't. My family has chosen to be in and out of the shower in ten minutes so that we don't use too much water.
47. This is a perfume commonly used for such purposes by shamans in the Peru. It may be placed in a sprayer bottle and sprayed around a room. The Andean custom of spraying it with the mouth is *not* recommended as the commercial perfume contains toxic wood alcohol! A safer alternative is Shaman's Market Organic Floral Water specifically marketed for this oral method of spraying called "phukuy." It is available through the Shaman's Market website at *www.shamansmarket.com.*
48. The larch was seen as the most sacred of all the trees. Perhaps this is because the larch is the only evergreen that loses its needles and appears to die in the autumn only to come back to life again in springtime.
49. In the Ulchi tradition, men must be on their knees with their hands in a prayer position and touch the ground with their forehead three times. Women may either kneel (a woman's forehead does not touch the ground) or bow while standing; however, they must have a stick across the ground in front of them for protection as they perform the offering ritual. This stems from the belief that animals are powerful "people" and since they are so closely related to us are capable of mating with humans! No stick is necessary when women make offerings inside as the indoor or house spirits are all female.
50. This offering of alcohol—particularly clear or white spirits—is common to many other shamanic traditions as well. For instance, the Peruvian people use drinks such as pisco or white rum. On the steppes of Central Asia in Tuva, fermented mare's milk is the preferred offering beverage. All across Siberia, vodka is the chosen offering to the spirits. If you prefer not to use alcohol, use a clear or white beverage such as white grape juice or ordinary milk, and

rather than flicking it around, simply leave a small bowl of it on your altar.

51. Offerings never include meat as animals are considered people, and a meat offering would imply that the Ulchi thought the spirits were cannibals! In the same vein, the waters are also never given vodka.

52. To offer milk, the Tuvans typically use a "nine-eyed throwing spoon." Nine is a particularly sacred number to the Tuvan people, and so this object is a special spoon with nine smaller compartments carved into in its bowl.

53. A video interview, titled "Interview Bhola Nath Banstola," of Bhola may be found on *youtube.com*.

54. In cases when serious illnesses are being addressed, a red cloth may be used. Red is a highly sacred color among the Nepalese, and so in that case, the mandala is effectively "held" in a protective field.

55. Puma and his grandfather are Quechua Indians from Chinchero, which lies in the sacred Incan valley near Cusco. Their people's roots go back to the very ancient Chavin culture that lived in the north coast foothill region of Peru.

56. Puma always places ingredients for the *despacho* in a clockwise fashion with his right hand. This is the direction and hand used for ceremonies of creating and focusing energy. Conversely, Andean cultures use the counterclockwise direction for unwinding and unmaking rituals.

57. Michael Winkelman, "Trance States: A Theoretical Model and Cross-Cultural Analysis," *Ethos,* 14/2 (Summer, 1986), 174–203, published by Blackwell Publishing on behalf of the American Anthropological Association. Stable URL: *http://www.jstor.org/stable/639951* accessed: 30/03/2010 16:03.

58. Ibid., 198.

59. Ibid., 178.

60. This is a term used by Dr. Michael Harner, PhD, founder of the Foundation for Shamanic Studies, to characterize the state of awareness achieved through shamanic journeying.

61. From an episode of the National Public Radio program *All Things Considered*, which aired on August 11, 2010. A transcript may be found at: *http://www.npr.org/templates/story/story.php?storyId=129083762&sc=emaf.*

62. Instructions on making your shamanic implements of power may be found in the companion book, *A Spirit Walker's Guide to Shamanic Implements*, available through *www.myspiritwalk.com*.

63. In this work, the singers produce pure tones that are remarkably similar to the sounds that are usually only possible with an electronic synthesizer—a form of music for which Stockhausen was well known.

64. This article is now found in the public domain and may be downloaded at: *http://www.docstoc.com/docs/21849609/Overtone-Singing-Throat-Singing*.

65. It is useful to note here that across the Siberian/Central Asian region, shamans also play the mouth/jaw harp or *khomus* to accompany their overtone chanting. Tones created by this instrument are also produced by changing the resonating shape of the mouth and/or throat and may be used to mimic nature sounds.

66. This practice has two major forms. In *apyromantic scapulimancy*, the scapula of a freshly killed animal is read for information. This style of divination was widespread across Europe, North Africa, and the Near East and is still practiced in isolated regions of eastern Europe today. In *pyromantic scapulimancy* the patterns created when the bone is burned in a fire are interpreted. This method has been preserved in the traditions of the Japanese Shinto religion, which itself has seemingly preserved threads of older shamanic cultures from the eastern Asian region. In Shinto, this form of divination is called *rokuboku*. During a *rokuboku* ritual, the shapes of cracking that appear when the scapula of an animal or a tortoiseshell is heated are read to determine the spirits' will.

67. While the name *nisse* is used in Norway and Denmark, the same spirits are referred to as *tomte* in Swedish and *tonttu* in Finnish.

68. Evelyn Rysdyk, "Wild and Green," *Sacred Hoop Magazine 65* (2009): 26–29.

69. Ibid.

70. Juha Janunen, "Tracing the Bear Myth in Northeast Asia," *Acta Slavica Iaponica* (Slavic Research Center, Hokkaido University, 2003). An English language version of this article may be found online at *tp://src-home.slav.hokudai.ac.jp/publictn/acta/20/asi20-001-janhunen.pdf*.

71. Natalia Fedorova, "Bronze castings of western Siberia," in *The Archaeology of Shamanism* edited by Neil Price (London and New York: Routledge/Taylor & Francis Group, 2001), 63.
72. Paul Shepard & Barry Sanders, *The Sacred Paw, The Bear in Nature, Myth and Literature* (New York: Viking Penguin, Inc., 1985), 88–89.
73. Some people may believe that it isn't necessary to feed birds when there is more abundant natural food. However, bird specialists at the Cornell University Ornithology Department keep their feeders filled year-round. This benefits not only the birds, but other animals who will visit the food source, too. And if you are very lucky, you may glimpse natural predators such as hawks, foxes, minks, and other predators as they become attracted by an increase in bird activity.
74. Scientists have discovered that a plant uses nearly 100 percent of the photons that hit the surface of its leaves and converts them into energy. Nothing is wasted. In addition, this conversion is done by the plant's proteins at the speed of a millionth of a millionth of a second! The plants aren't just highly effective solar energy converters, they are incredibly fast, as well. This was reported by the National Science Foundation on May 7, 2007. The complete press release may be found at *http://www.nsf.gov/news/news_summ. jsp?cntn_id=108534.*
75. Watson, *Gifts of Unknown Things, A True Story of Nature, Healing and Initiation from Indonesia's "Dancing Island."*
76. There are two reliable websites that offer comprehensive lists of shamanic healers. The first site, *www.shamanicteachers.com/practitioners.html*, includes those who were taught by Sandra Ingerman. The second listing has practitioners from many different traditions: *www.shamanlinks.net/Shaman_Links.htm.*
77. The author's own hour-long shamanic journey drumming CD may be purchased as either a physical CD or as download files: *www. spiritpassages.com/spiritpassagesstore.html.*
78. Instructions for making sacred bundles and medicine bags may be found in the companion book, *A Spirit Walker's Guide to Shamanic Implements*, available through *www.myspiritwalk.com.*

79. Sandra Ingerman's book, *Medicine for the Earth* (New York: Three Rivers Press, 2000), has detailed information on this work.
80. At the time of this writing (August 8, 2011), the world population was 6,954,238, 269. The square root of 1 percent of 7 billion is 8,366.60 people.
81. Proposed by Abraham Maslow in his 1943 paper, "A Theory of Human Motivation."

About the Author

© Kevin Brusie

Evelyn C. Rysdyk is a shamanic practitioner and teacher. She has studied with Michael Harner and Sandra Ingerman and is a graduate of the Foundation for Shamanic Studies Three-Year Program in Advanced Shamanism and Shamanic Healing. Since that time, she has worked with indigenous shamans from Siberia, Peru, Central Asia, and Nepal. Evelyn helped found True North, an integrated medical center in Falmouth, Maine, where she works alongside medical practitioners to bring physical, spiritual, emotional, and spiritual healing to patients. She lives in Maine. Visit her at *www.spiritpassages.com*.

To Our Readers

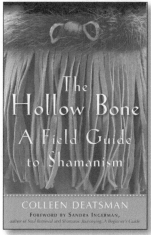
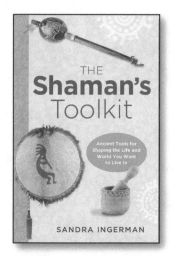